SHORTCOMINGS

SHORT

NAME: Miko Hayashi
AGE: 31
HEIGHT: 5' 4"
BORN: Cambridge, MA

NAME: Alice Kim
AGE: 29
HEIGHT: 5' 2"
BORN: Incheon, South Korea

NAME: Meredith Lee
AGE: 32
HEIGHT: 5' 5"
BORN: Los Angeles, CA

ADRIAN TOMINE

COMINGS

NAME: Sasha Lenz
AGE: 28
HEIGHT: 5' 8"
BORN: Benicia, CA

NAME: Autumn Phelps
AGE: 22
HEIGHT: 5' 7"
BORN: Tacoma, WA

NAME: Ben Tanaka
AGE: 30
HEIGHT: 5' 8"
BORN: Corvallis, OR

DRAWN AND QUARTERLY

ALSO BY ADRIAN TOMINE

32 Stories: The Complete Optic Nerve *Mini-Comics*

Sleepwalk and Other Stories

Summer Blonde

Scrapbook (Uncollected Work: 1990–2004)

Scenes from an Impending Marriage

New York Drawings

Killing and Dying

This story was originally serialized in issues nine through eleven of *Optic Nerve*, published by Drawn & Quarterly. The characters and events depicted in this book are fictitious. Any similarities to real persons, living or dead, is coincidental and not intended by the author.

drawnandquarterly.com
adrian-tomine.com

First hardcover edition: September 2007
Second hardcover printing: December 2007
First paperback edition: April 2009
Second paperback printing: March 2010
Third paperback printing: October 2012
Fourth paperback printing: November 2015

Printed in Canada

10 9 8 7 6 5 4

Library and Archives Canada Cataloguing in Publication
Tomine, Adrian, 1974–
Shortcomings / Adrian Tomine.
ISBN 978-1-897299-75-3
I.Title.
PN6727.T65S46 2009 741.5'973 C2008-907606-0

Published in the USA by Drawn & Quarterly, a client publisher of Farrar, Straus and Giroux. Orders: 888.330.8477

Published in Canada by Drawn & Quarterly, a client publisher of Raincoast Books. Orders: 800.663.5714

FOR SARAH

CHAPTER ONE

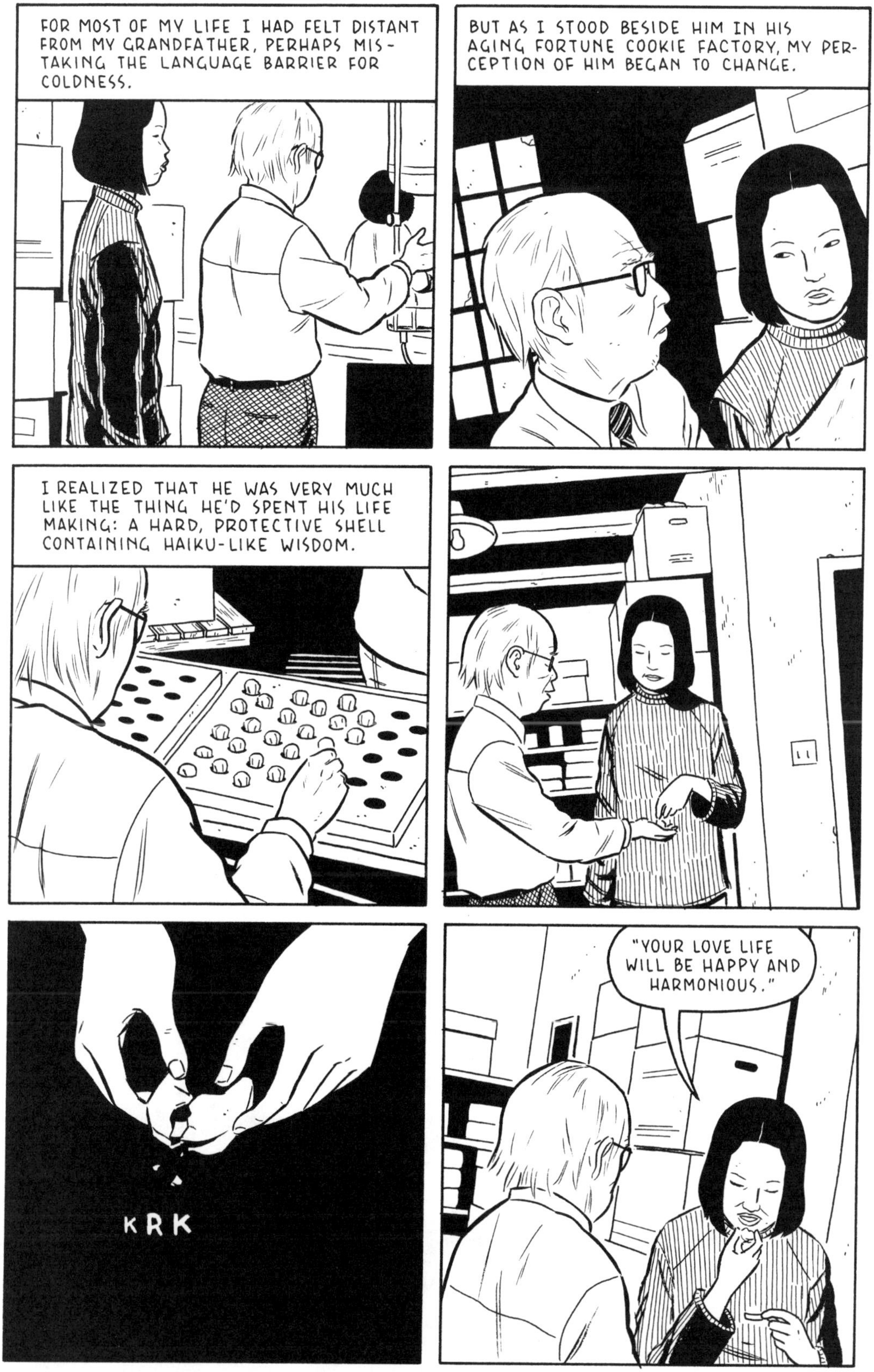

FOR MOST OF MY LIFE I HAD FELT DISTANT FROM MY GRANDFATHER, PERHAPS MIS-TAKING THE LANGUAGE BARRIER FOR COLDNESS.
BUT AS I STOOD BESIDE HIM IN HIS AGING FORTUNE COOKIE FACTORY, MY PER-CEPTION OF HIM BEGAN TO CHANGE.
I REALIZED THAT HE WAS VERY MUCH LIKE THE THING HE'D SPENT HIS LIFE MAKING: A HARD, PROTECTIVE SHELL CONTAINING HAIKU-LIKE WISDOM.
KRK
"YOUR LOVE LIFE WILL BE HAPPY AND HARMONIOUS."

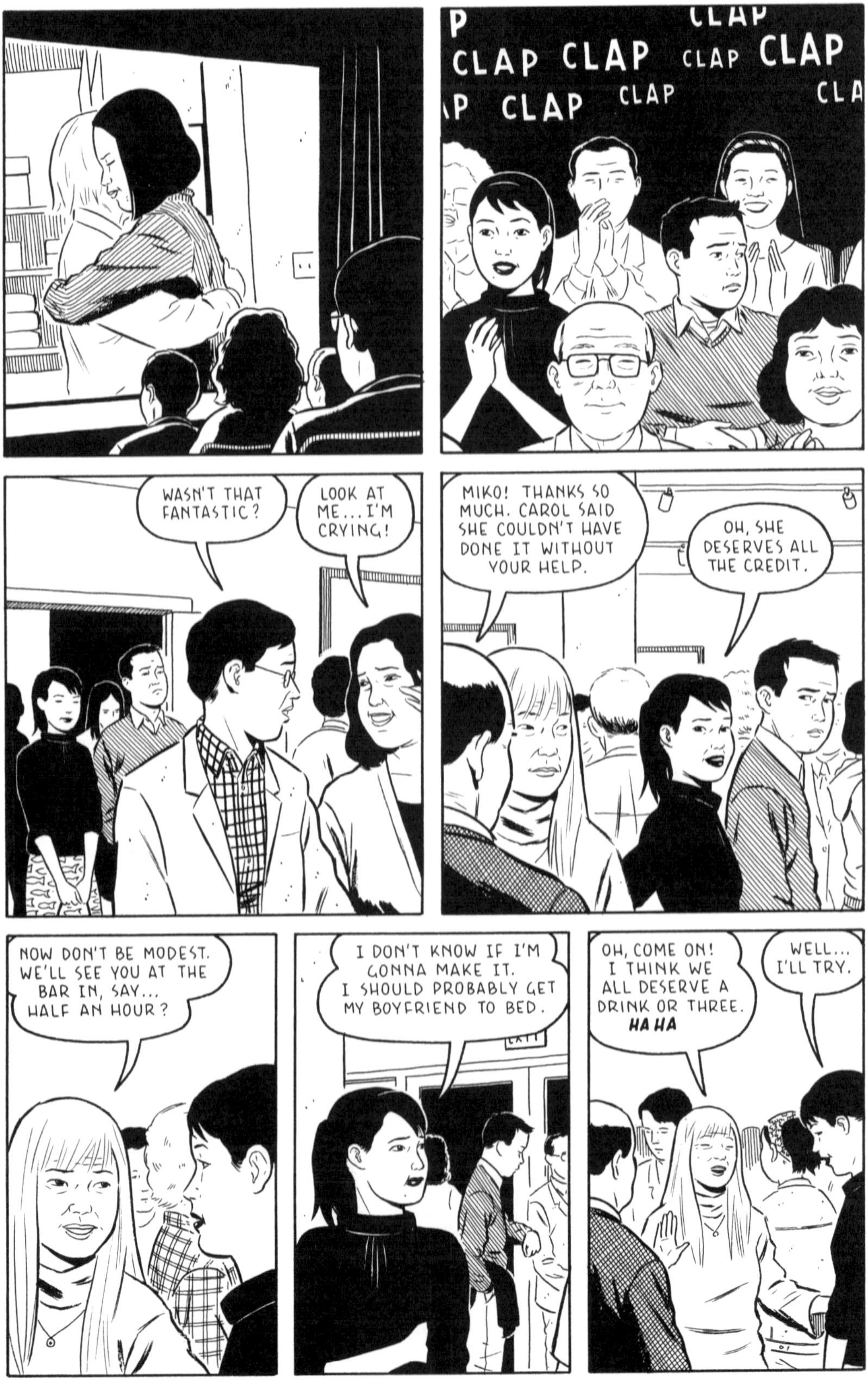
P CLAP
CLAP CLAP CLAP CLAP
P CLAP CLAP CLA
WASN'T THAT FANTASTIC?
LOOK AT ME... I'M CRYING!
MIKO! THANKS SO MUCH. CAROL SAID SHE COULDN'T HAVE DONE IT WITHOUT YOUR HELP.
OH, SHE DESERVES ALL THE CREDIT.
NOW DON'T BE MODEST. WE'LL SEE YOU AT THE BAR IN, SAY... HALF AN HOUR?
I DON'T KNOW IF I'M GONNA MAKE IT. I SHOULD PROBABLY GET MY BOYFRIEND TO BED.
OH, COME ON! I THINK WE ALL DESERVE A DRINK OR THREE.
HA HA
WELL... I'LL TRY.

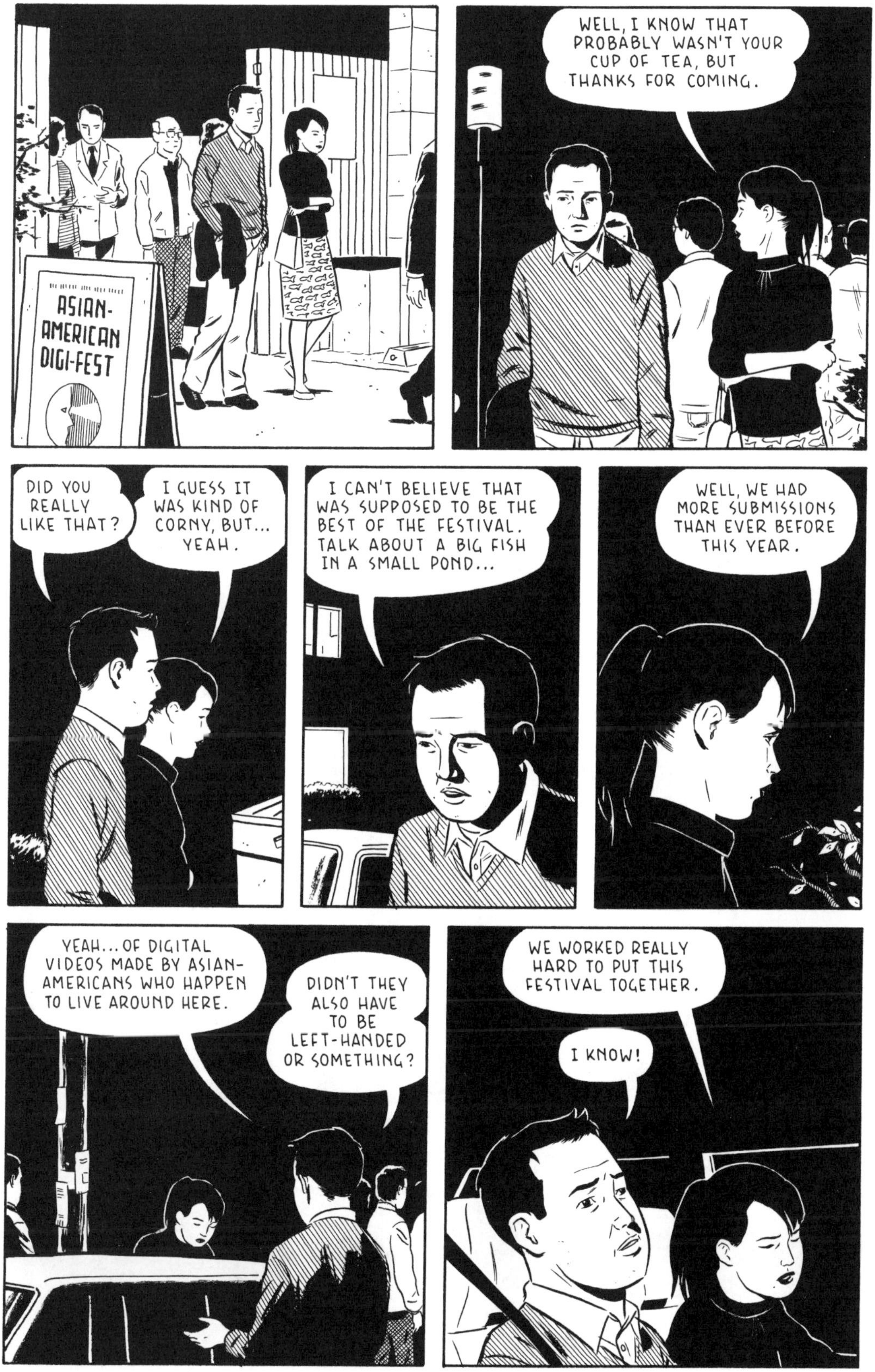
ASIAN-AMERICAN DIGI-FEST
WELL, I KNOW THAT PROBABLY WASN'T YOUR CUP OF TEA, BUT THANKS FOR COMING.
DID YOU REALLY LIKE THAT?
I GUESS IT WAS KIND OF CORNY, BUT... YEAH.
I CAN'T BELIEVE THAT WAS SUPPOSED TO BE THE BEST OF THE FESTIVAL. TALK ABOUT A BIG FISH IN A SMALL POND...
WELL, WE HAD MORE SUBMISSIONS THAN EVER BEFORE THIS YEAR.
YEAH... OF DIGITAL VIDEOS MADE BY ASIAN-AMERICANS WHO HAPPEN TO LIVE AROUND HERE.
DIDN'T THEY ALSO HAVE TO BE LEFT-HANDED OR SOMETHING?
WE WORKED REALLY HARD TO PUT THIS FESTIVAL TOGETHER.
I KNOW!

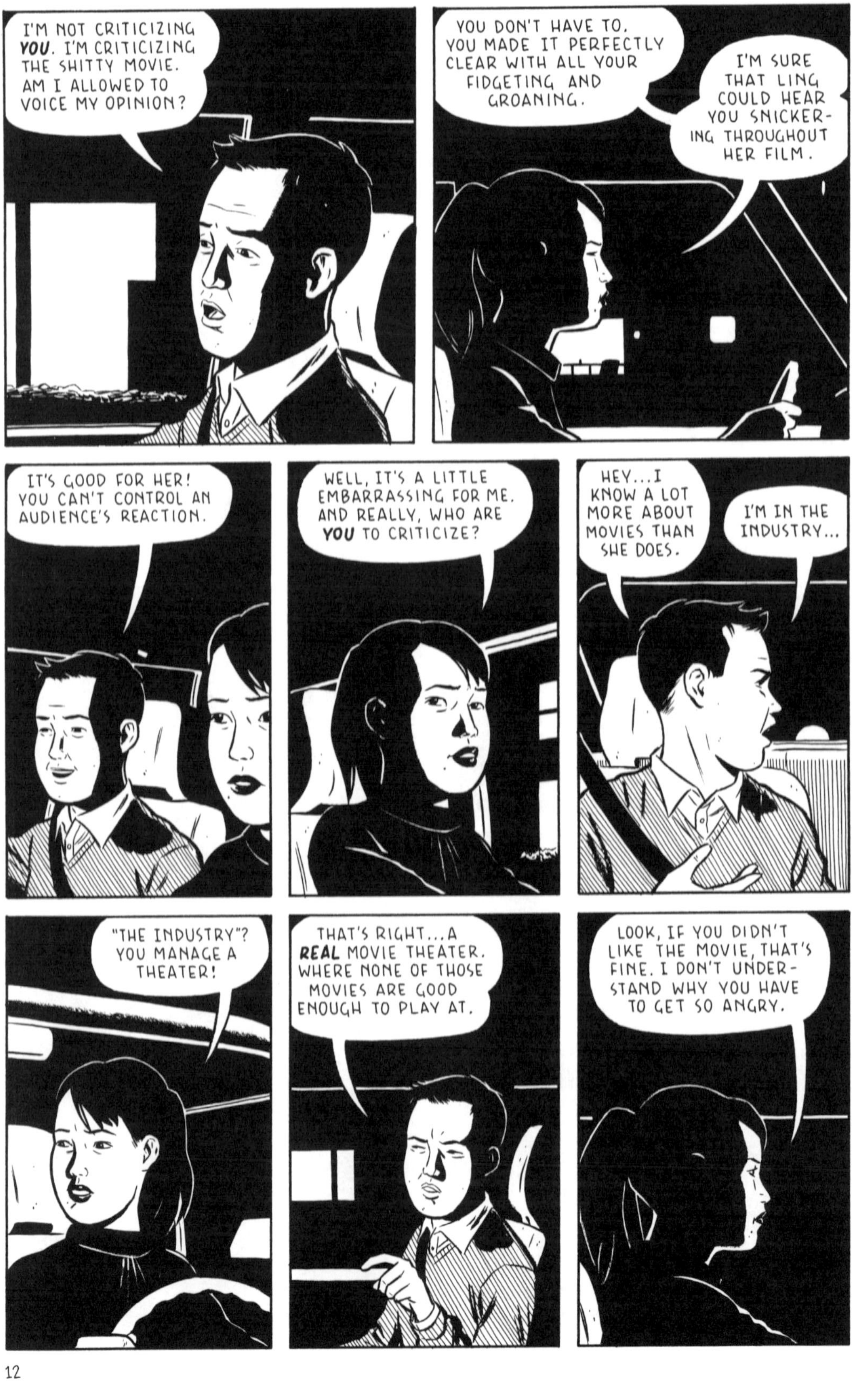
I'M NOT CRITICIZING **YOU**. I'M CRITICIZING THE SHITTY MOVIE. AM I ALLOWED TO VOICE MY OPINION?
YOU DON'T HAVE TO. YOU MADE IT PERFECTLY CLEAR WITH ALL YOUR FIDGETING AND GROANING.
I'M SURE THAT LING COULD HEAR YOU SNICKERING THROUGHOUT HER FILM.
IT'S GOOD FOR HER! YOU CAN'T CONTROL AN AUDIENCE'S REACTION.
WELL, IT'S A LITTLE EMBARRASSING FOR ME. AND REALLY, WHO ARE **YOU** TO CRITICIZE?
HEY... I KNOW A LOT MORE ABOUT MOVIES THAN SHE DOES.
I'M IN THE INDUSTRY...
"THE INDUSTRY"? YOU MANAGE A THEATER!
THAT'S RIGHT... A **REAL** MOVIE THEATER. WHERE NONE OF THOSE MOVIES ARE GOOD ENOUGH TO PLAY AT.
LOOK, IF YOU DIDN'T LIKE THE MOVIE, THAT'S FINE. I DON'T UNDERSTAND WHY YOU HAVE TO GET SO ANGRY.

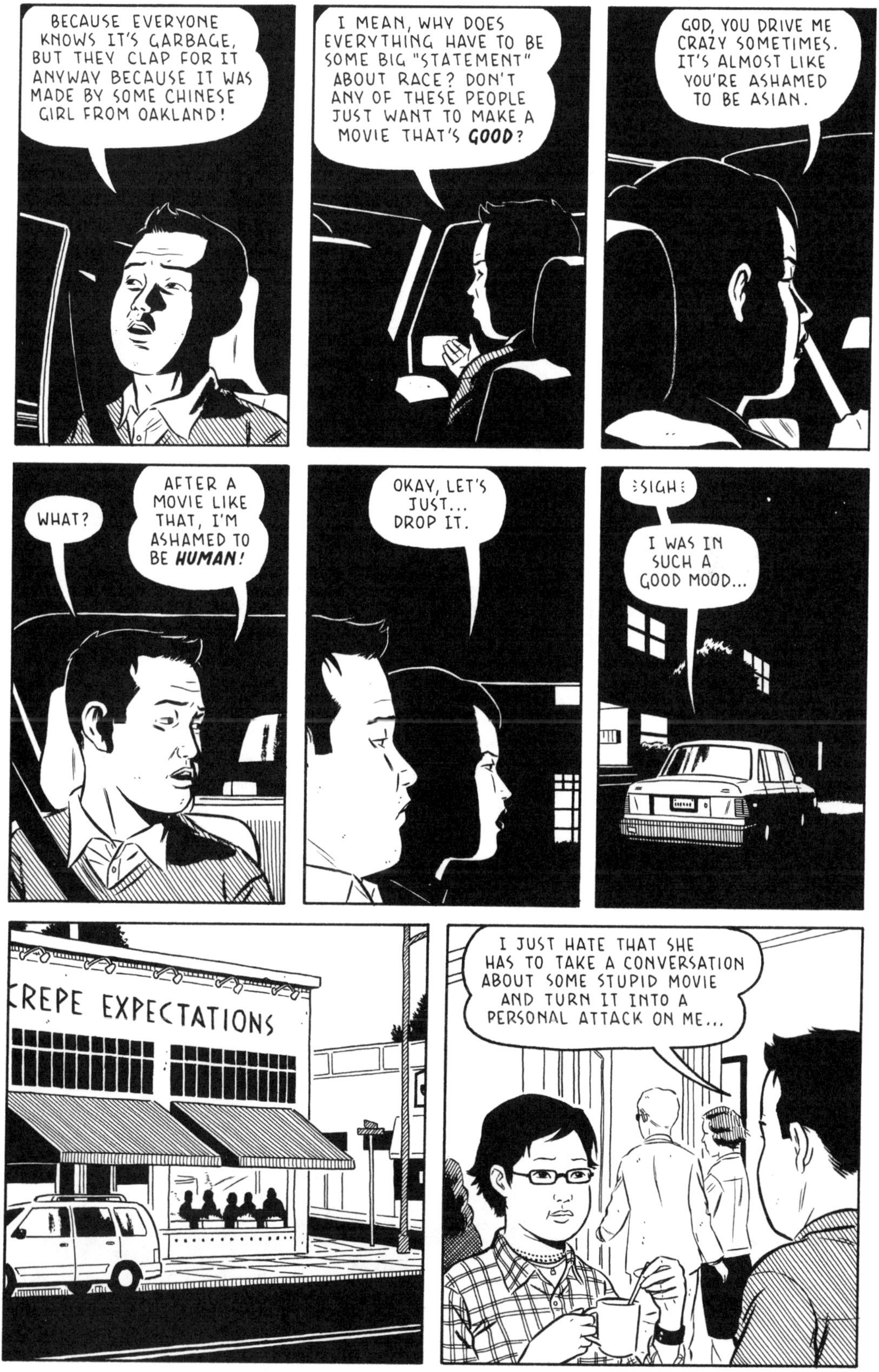
BECAUSE EVERYONE KNOWS IT'S GARBAGE, BUT THEY CLAP FOR IT ANYWAY BECAUSE IT WAS MADE BY SOME CHINESE GIRL FROM OAKLAND!
I MEAN, WHY DOES EVERYTHING HAVE TO BE SOME BIG "STATEMENT" ABOUT RACE? DON'T ANY OF THESE PEOPLE JUST WANT TO MAKE A MOVIE THAT'S **GOOD**?
GOD, YOU DRIVE ME CRAZY SOMETIMES. IT'S ALMOST LIKE YOU'RE ASHAMED TO BE ASIAN.
WHAT?
AFTER A MOVIE LIKE THAT, I'M ASHAMED TO BE **HUMAN**!
OKAY, LET'S JUST... DROP IT.
SIGH
I WAS IN SUCH A GOOD MOOD...
CREPE EXPECTATIONS
I JUST HATE THAT SHE HAS TO TAKE A CONVERSATION ABOUT SOME STUPID MOVIE AND TURN IT INTO A PERSONAL ATTACK ON ME...

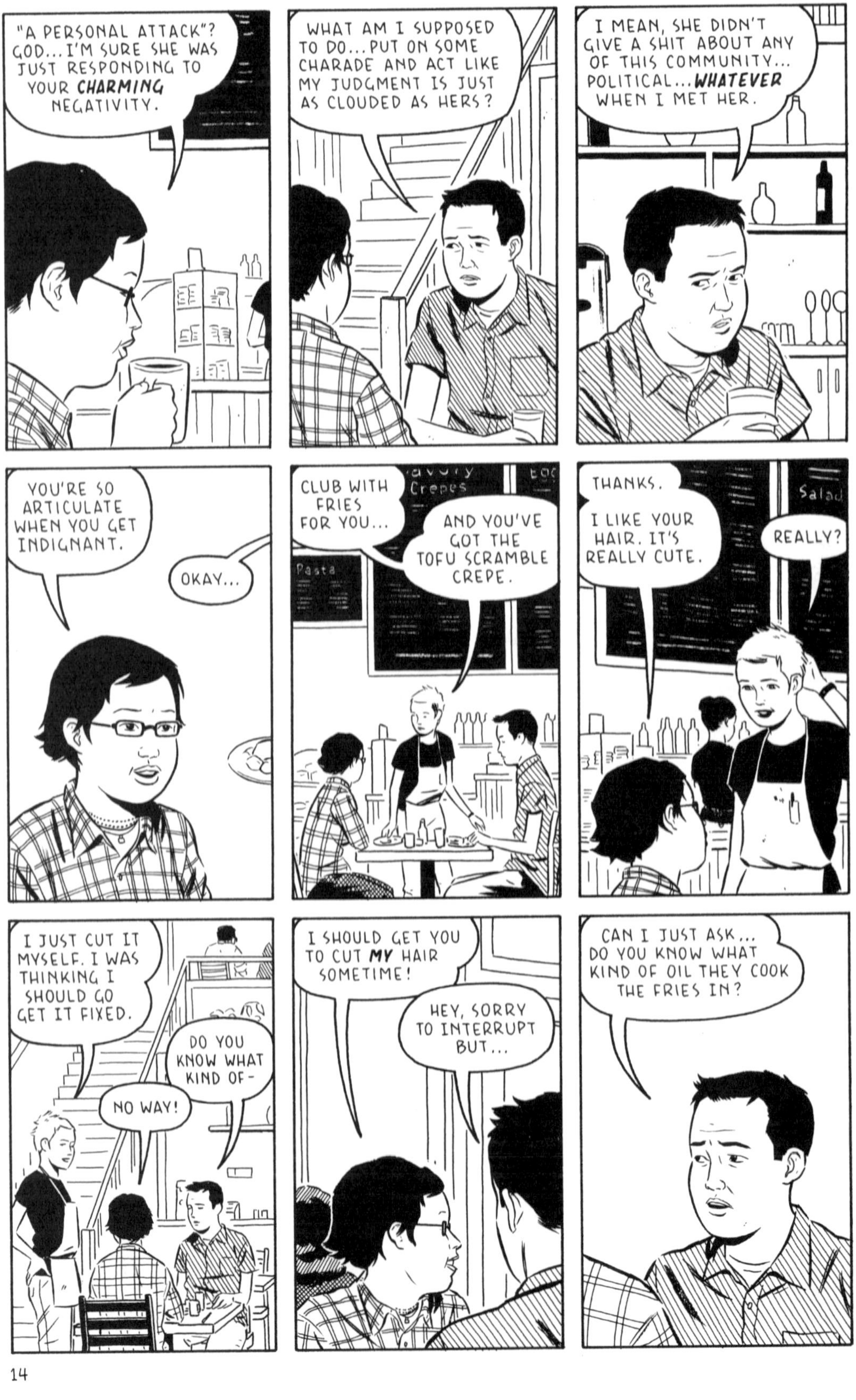
"A PERSONAL ATTACK"? GOD... I'M SURE SHE WAS JUST RESPONDING TO YOUR **CHARMING** NEGATIVITY.
WHAT AM I SUPPOSED TO DO... PUT ON SOME CHARADE AND ACT LIKE MY JUDGMENT IS JUST AS CLOUDED AS HERS?
I MEAN, SHE DIDN'T GIVE A SHIT ABOUT ANY OF THIS COMMUNITY... POLITICAL... **WHATEVER** WHEN I MET HER.
YOU'RE SO ARTICULATE WHEN YOU GET INDIGNANT.
OKAY...
Crepes
CLUB WITH FRIES FOR YOU...
AND YOU'VE GOT THE TOFU SCRAMBLE CREPE.
Pasta
THANKS.
Salad
I LIKE YOUR HAIR. IT'S REALLY CUTE.
REALLY?
I JUST CUT IT MYSELF. I WAS THINKING I SHOULD GO GET IT FIXED.
DO YOU KNOW WHAT KIND OF-
NO WAY!
I SHOULD GET YOU TO CUT **MY** HAIR SOMETIME!
HEY, SORRY TO INTERRUPT BUT...
CAN I JUST ASK... DO YOU KNOW WHAT KIND OF OIL THEY COOK THE FRIES IN?

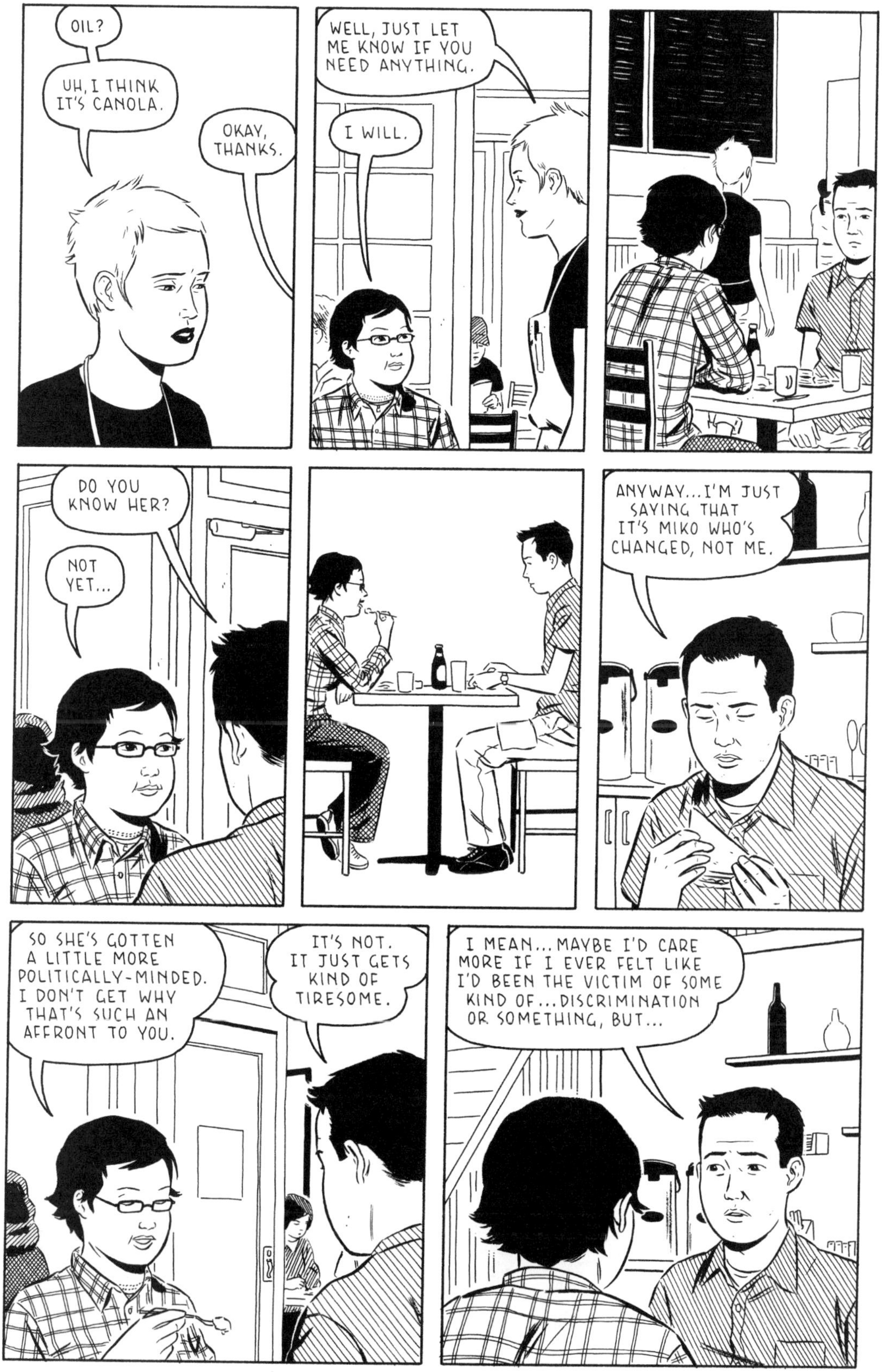

OIL?
UH, I THINK IT'S CANOLA.
OKAY, THANKS.
WELL, JUST LET ME KNOW IF YOU NEED ANYTHING.
I WILL.
DO YOU KNOW HER?
NOT YET...
ANYWAY... I'M JUST SAYING THAT IT'S MIKO WHO'S CHANGED, NOT ME.
SO SHE'S GOTTEN A LITTLE MORE POLITICALLY-MINDED. I DON'T GET WHY THAT'S SUCH AN AFFRONT TO YOU.
IT'S NOT. IT JUST GETS KIND OF TIRESOME.
I MEAN... MAYBE I'D CARE MORE IF I EVER FELT LIKE I'D BEEN THE VICTIM OF SOME KIND OF... DISCRIMINATION OR SOMETHING, BUT...

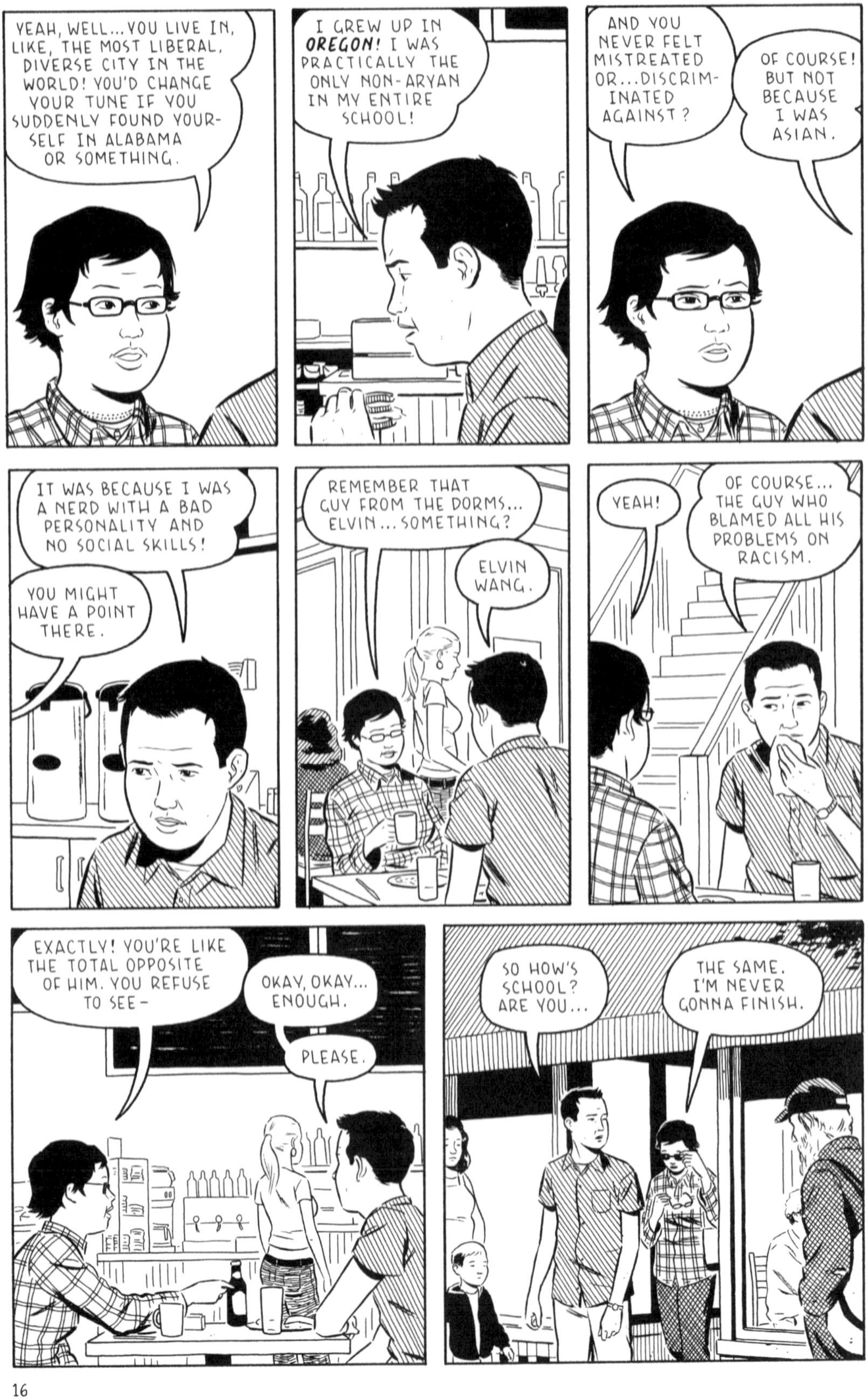
YEAH, WELL... YOU LIVE IN, LIKE, THE MOST LIBERAL, DIVERSE CITY IN THE WORLD! YOU'D CHANGE YOUR TUNE IF YOU SUDDENLY FOUND YOURSELF IN ALABAMA OR SOMETHING.
I GREW UP IN **OREGON**! I WAS PRACTICALLY THE ONLY NON-ARYAN IN MY ENTIRE SCHOOL!
AND YOU NEVER FELT MISTREATED OR... DISCRIMINATED AGAINST?
OF COURSE! BUT NOT BECAUSE I WAS ASIAN.
IT WAS BECAUSE I WAS A NERD WITH A BAD PERSONALITY AND NO SOCIAL SKILLS!
YOU MIGHT HAVE A POINT THERE.
REMEMBER THAT GUY FROM THE DORMS... ELVIN... SOMETHING?
ELVIN WANG.
YEAH!
OF COURSE... THE GUY WHO BLAMED ALL HIS PROBLEMS ON RACISM.
EXACTLY! YOU'RE LIKE THE TOTAL OPPOSITE OF HIM. YOU REFUSE TO SEE-
OKAY, OKAY... ENOUGH.
PLEASE.
SO HOW'S SCHOOL? ARE YOU...
THE SAME. I'M NEVER GONNA FINISH.

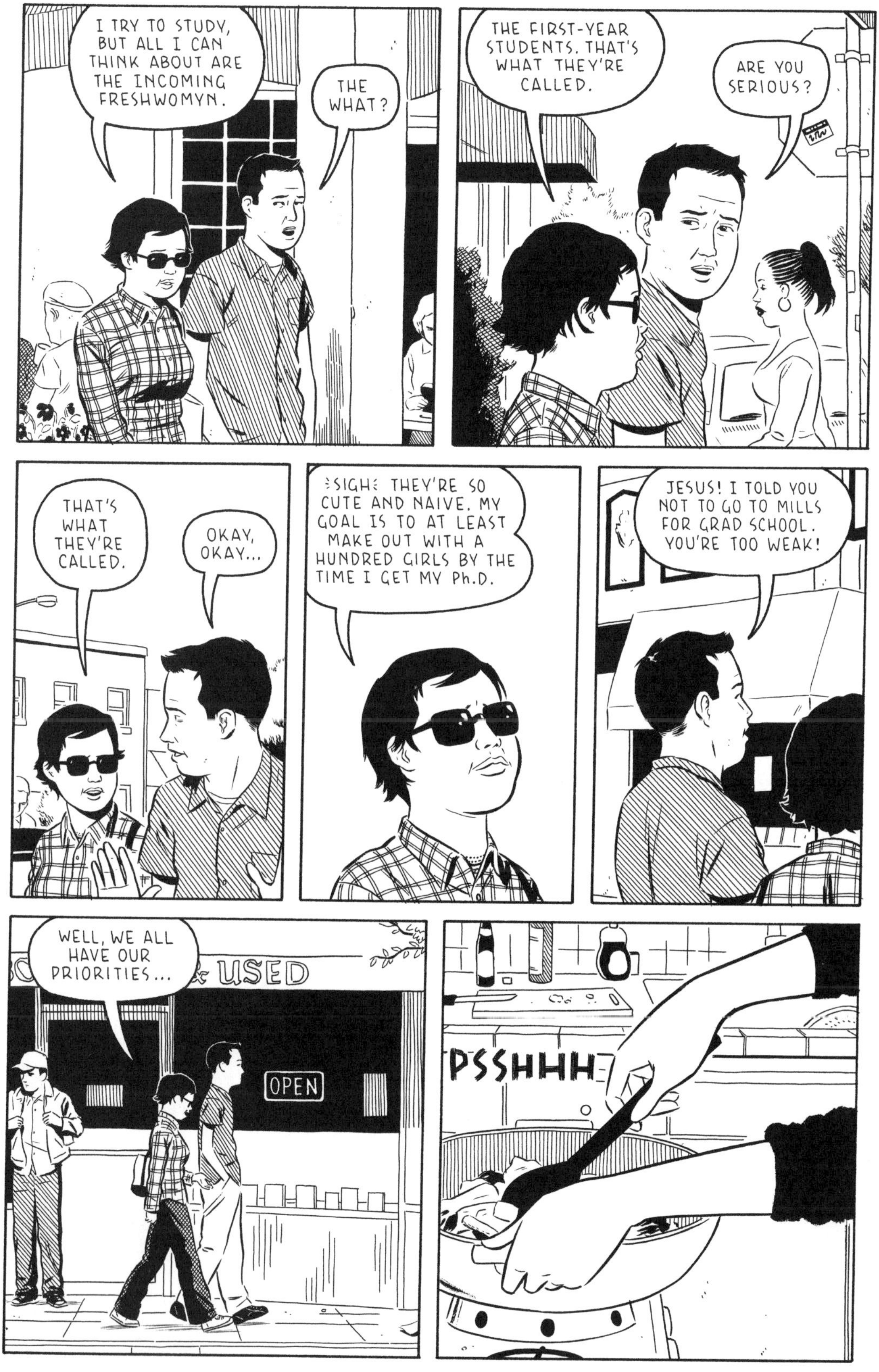

I TRY TO STUDY, BUT ALL I CAN THINK ABOUT ARE THE INCOMING FRESHWOMYN.
THE WHAT?
THE FIRST-YEAR STUDENTS. THAT'S WHAT THEY'RE CALLED.
ARE YOU SERIOUS?
THAT'S WHAT THEY'RE CALLED.
OKAY, OKAY...
SIGH THEY'RE SO CUTE AND NAIVE. MY GOAL IS TO AT LEAST MAKE OUT WITH A HUNDRED GIRLS BY THE TIME I GET MY Ph.D.
JESUS! I TOLD YOU NOT TO GO TO MILLS FOR GRAD SCHOOL. YOU'RE TOO WEAK!
WELL, WE ALL HAVE OUR PRIORITIES...
& USED
OPEN
PSSHHH

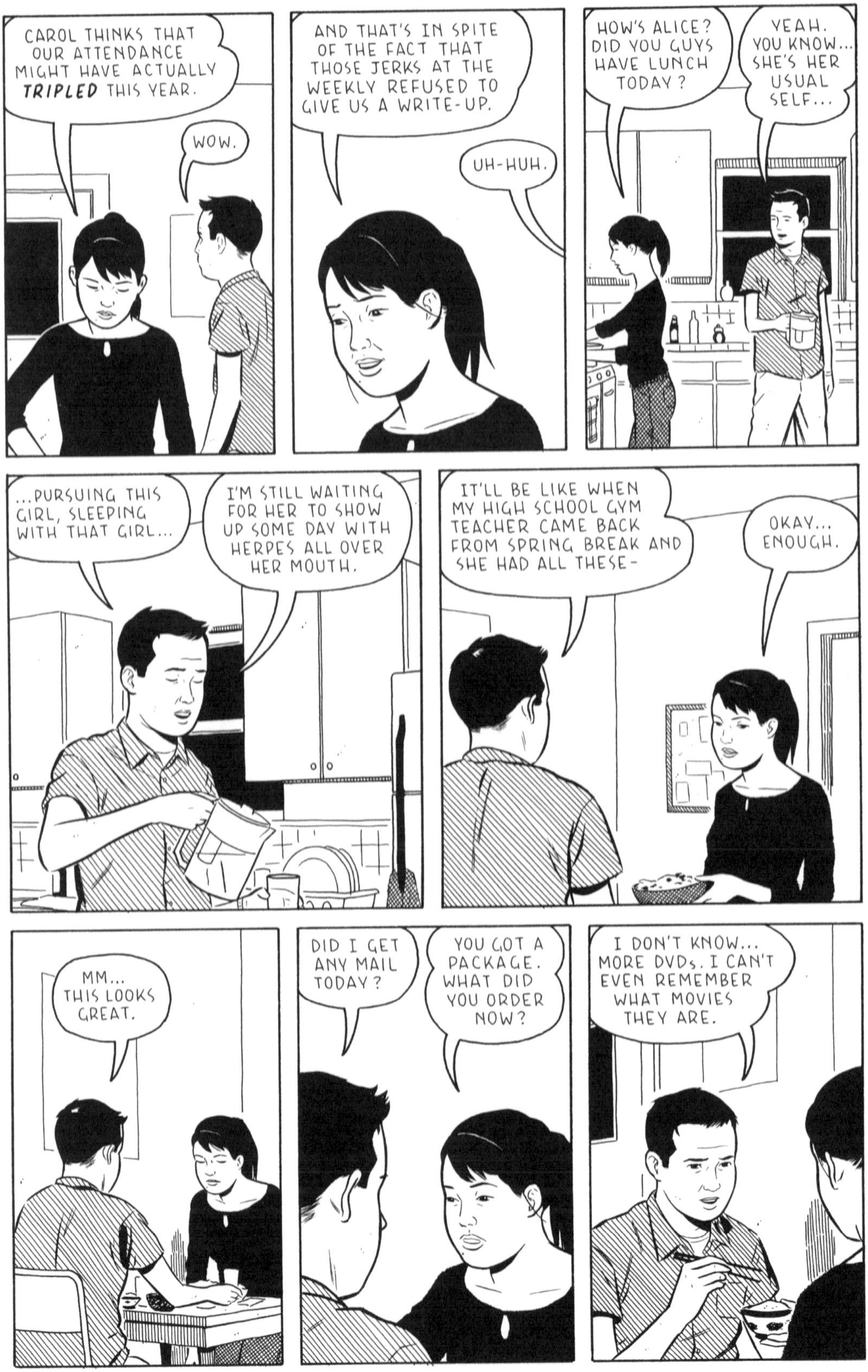
CAROL THINKS THAT OUR ATTENDANCE MIGHT HAVE ACTUALLY TRIPLED THIS YEAR.
WOW.
AND THAT'S IN SPITE OF THE FACT THAT THOSE JERKS AT THE WEEKLY REFUSED TO GIVE US A WRITE-UP.
UH-HUH.
HOW'S ALICE? DID YOU GUYS HAVE LUNCH TODAY?
YEAH. YOU KNOW... SHE'S HER USUAL SELF...
...PURSUING THIS GIRL, SLEEPING WITH THAT GIRL...
I'M STILL WAITING FOR HER TO SHOW UP SOME DAY WITH HERPES ALL OVER HER MOUTH.
IT'LL BE LIKE WHEN MY HIGH SCHOOL GYM TEACHER CAME BACK FROM SPRING BREAK AND SHE HAD ALL THESE-
OKAY... ENOUGH.
MM... THIS LOOKS GREAT.
DID I GET ANY MAIL TODAY?
YOU GOT A PACKAGE. WHAT DID YOU ORDER NOW?
I DON'T KNOW... MORE DVDs. I CAN'T EVEN REMEMBER WHAT MOVIES THEY ARE.

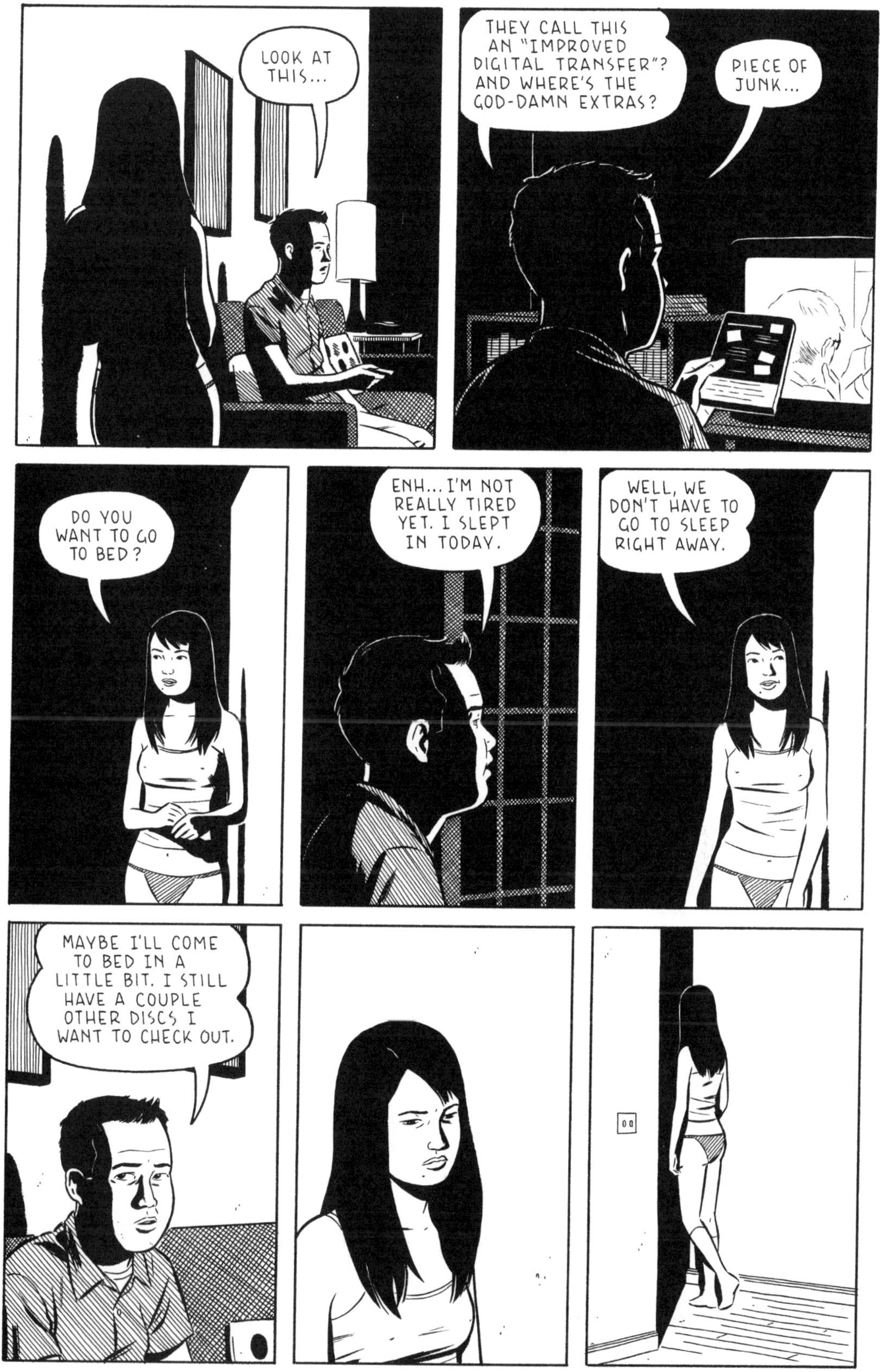
LOOK AT THIS...
THEY CALL THIS AN "IMPROVED DIGITAL TRANSFER"? AND WHERE'S THE GOD-DAMN EXTRAS?
PIECE OF JUNK...
DO YOU WANT TO GO TO BED?
ENH... I'M NOT REALLY TIRED YET. I SLEPT IN TODAY.
WELL, WE DON'T HAVE TO GO TO SLEEP RIGHT AWAY.
MAYBE I'LL COME TO BED IN A LITTLE BIT. I STILL HAVE A COUPLE OTHER DISCS I WANT TO CHECK OUT.

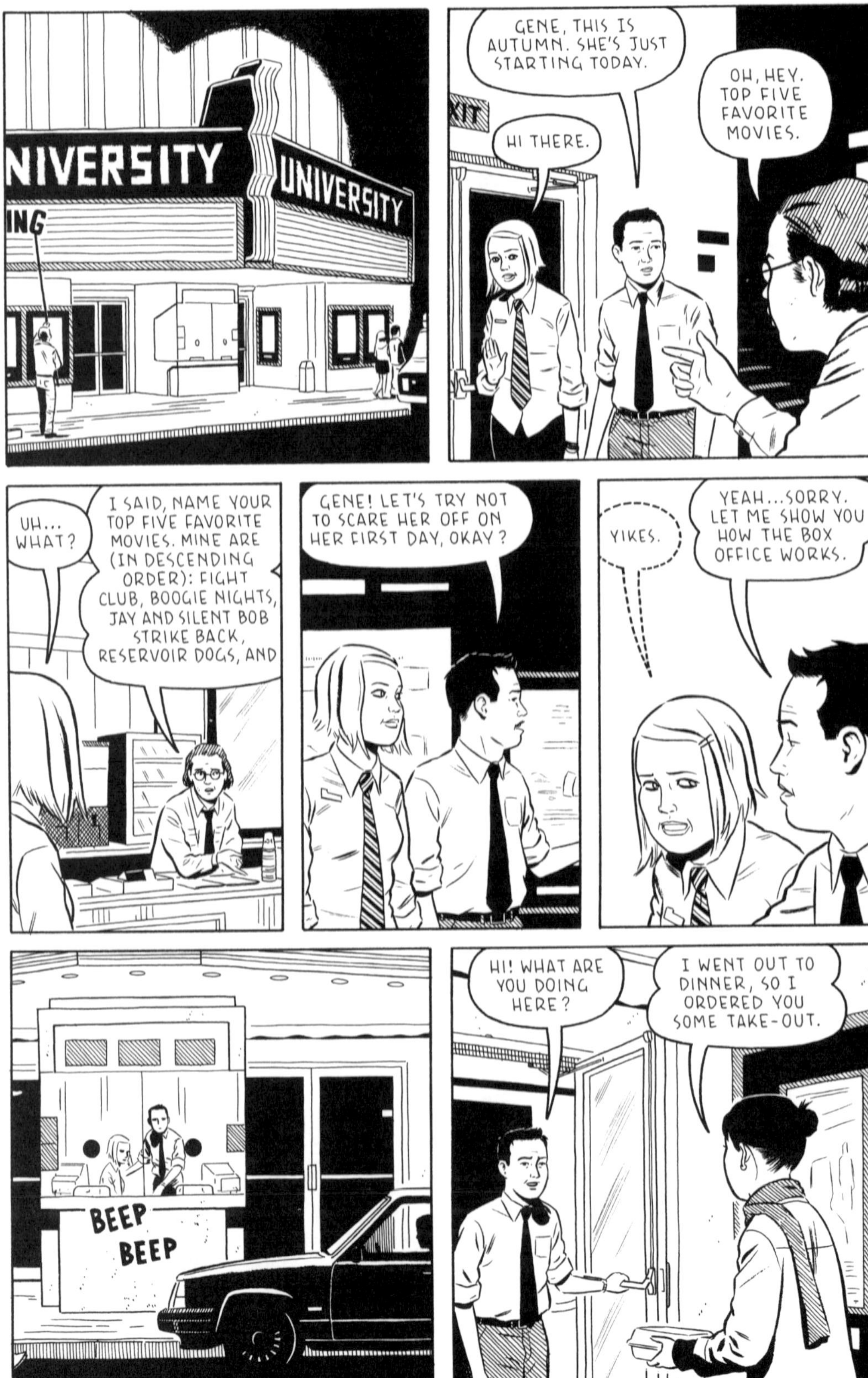
NIVERSITY
UNIVERSITY
ING
GENE, THIS IS AUTUMN. SHE'S JUST STARTING TODAY.
HI THERE.
OH, HEY. TOP FIVE FAVORITE MOVIES.
EXIT
UH... WHAT?
I SAID, NAME YOUR TOP FIVE FAVORITE MOVIES. MINE ARE (IN DESCENDING ORDER): FIGHT CLUB, BOOGIE NIGHTS, JAY AND SILENT BOB STRIKE BACK, RESERVOIR DOGS, AND
GENE! LET'S TRY NOT TO SCARE HER OFF ON HER FIRST DAY, OKAY?
YIKES.
YEAH...SORRY. LET ME SHOW YOU HOW THE BOX OFFICE WORKS.
BEEP
BEEP
HI! WHAT ARE YOU DOING HERE?
I WENT OUT TO DINNER, SO I ORDERED YOU SOME TAKE-OUT.

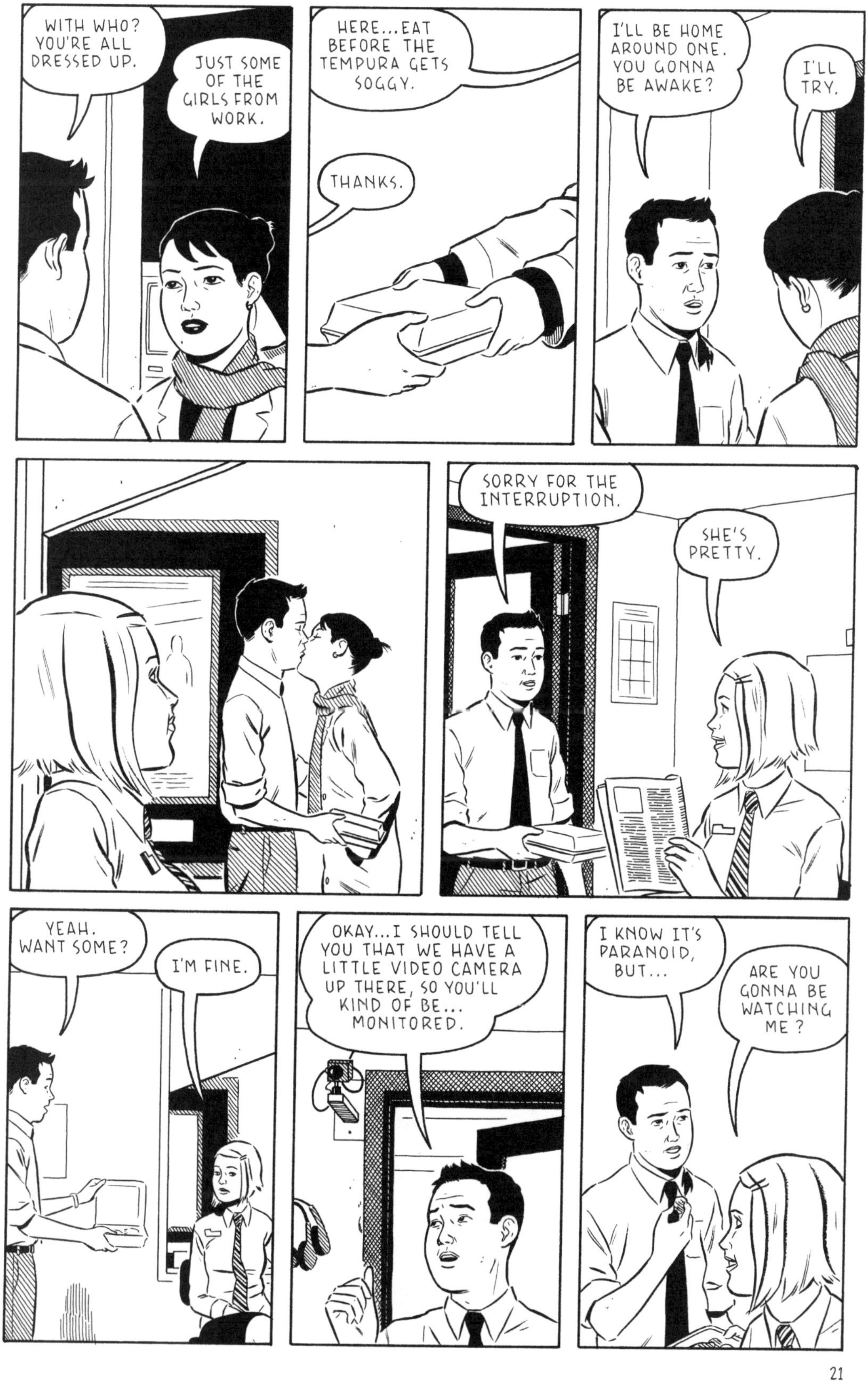
WITH WHO? YOU'RE ALL DRESSED UP.
JUST SOME OF THE GIRLS FROM WORK.
HERE... EAT BEFORE THE TEMPURA GETS SOGGY.
THANKS.
I'LL BE HOME AROUND ONE. YOU GONNA BE AWAKE?
I'LL TRY.
SORRY FOR THE INTERRUPTION.
SHE'S PRETTY.
YEAH. WANT SOME?
I'M FINE.
OKAY... I SHOULD TELL YOU THAT WE HAVE A LITTLE VIDEO CAMERA UP THERE, SO YOU'LL KIND OF BE... MONITORED.
I KNOW IT'S PARANOID, BUT...
ARE YOU GONNA BE WATCHING ME?

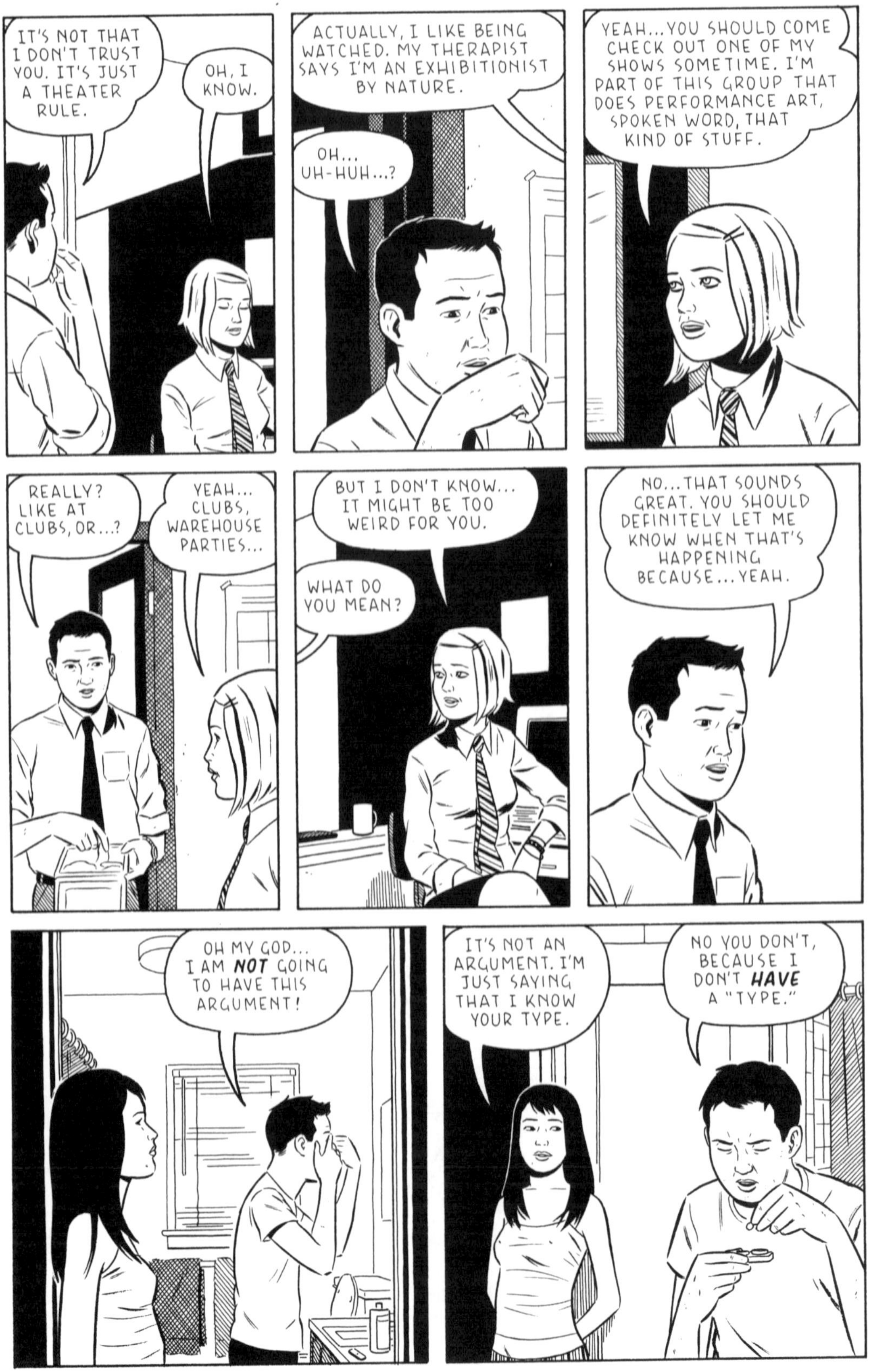
IT'S NOT THAT I DON'T TRUST YOU. IT'S JUST A THEATER RULE.
OH, I KNOW.
ACTUALLY, I LIKE BEING WATCHED. MY THERAPIST SAYS I'M AN EXHIBITIONIST BY NATURE.
OH... UH-HUH...?
YEAH... YOU SHOULD COME CHECK OUT ONE OF MY SHOWS SOMETIME. I'M PART OF THIS GROUP THAT DOES PERFORMANCE ART, SPOKEN WORD, THAT KIND OF STUFF.
REALLY? LIKE AT CLUBS, OR...?
YEAH... CLUBS, WAREHOUSE PARTIES...
BUT I DON'T KNOW... IT MIGHT BE TOO WEIRD FOR YOU.
WHAT DO YOU MEAN?
NO... THAT SOUNDS GREAT. YOU SHOULD DEFINITELY LET ME KNOW WHEN THAT'S HAPPENING BECAUSE... YEAH.
OH MY GOD... I AM **NOT** GOING TO HAVE THIS ARGUMENT!
IT'S NOT AN ARGUMENT. I'M JUST SAYING THAT I KNOW YOUR TYPE.
NO YOU DON'T, BECAUSE I DON'T **HAVE** A "TYPE."

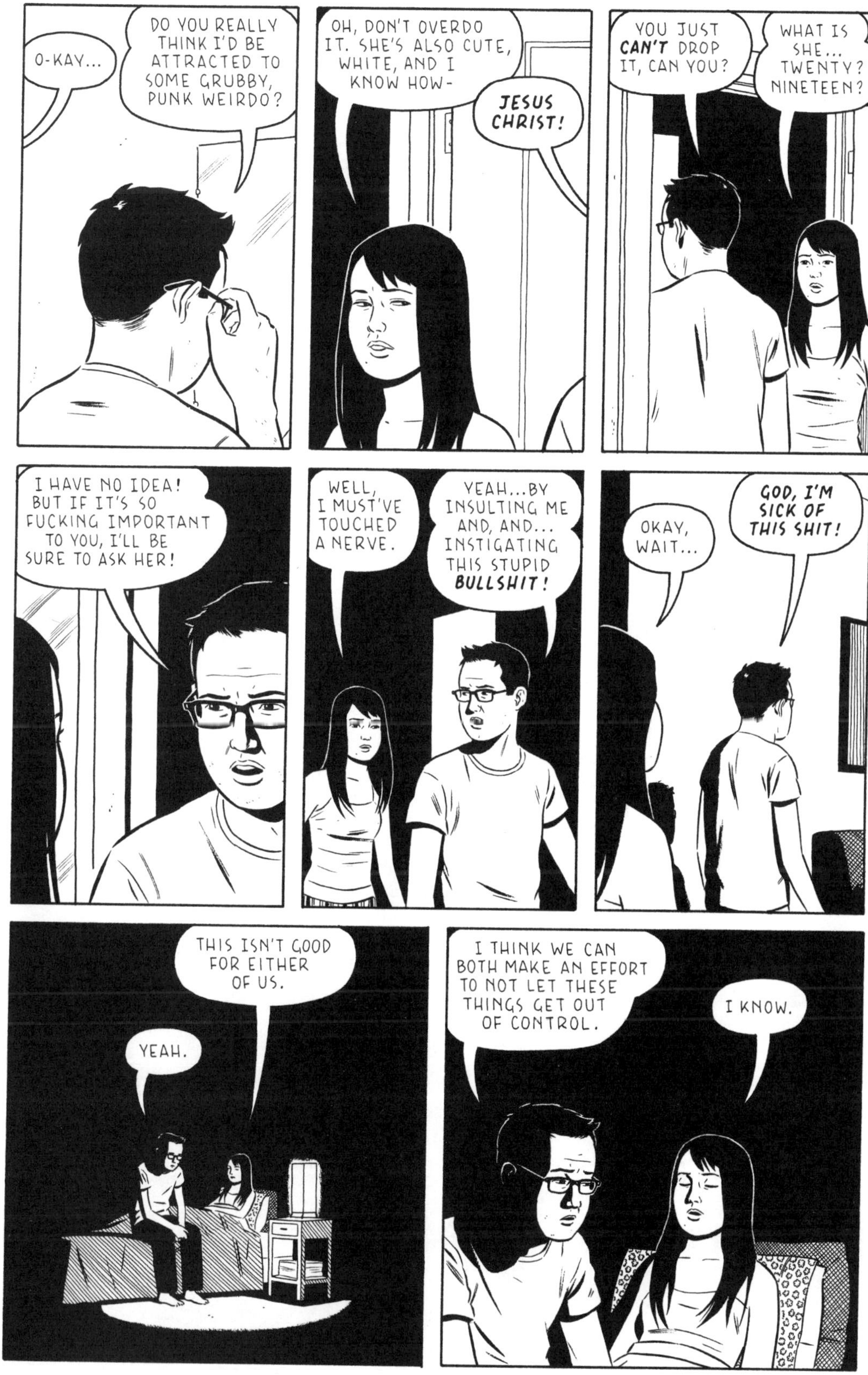
O-KAY...
DO YOU REALLY THINK I'D BE ATTRACTED TO SOME GRUBBY, PUNK WEIRDO?
OH, DON'T OVERDO IT. SHE'S ALSO CUTE, WHITE, AND I KNOW HOW-
JESUS CHRIST!
YOU JUST CAN'T DROP IT, CAN YOU?
WHAT IS SHE... TWENTY? NINETEEN?
I HAVE NO IDEA! BUT IF IT'S SO FUCKING IMPORTANT TO YOU, I'LL BE SURE TO ASK HER!
WELL, I MUST'VE TOUCHED A NERVE.
YEAH...BY INSULTING ME AND, AND... INSTIGATING THIS STUPID BULLSHIT!
OKAY, WAIT...
GOD, I'M SICK OF THIS SHIT!
YEAH.
THIS ISN'T GOOD FOR EITHER OF US.
I THINK WE CAN BOTH MAKE AN EFFORT TO NOT LET THESE THINGS GET OUT OF CONTROL.
I KNOW.

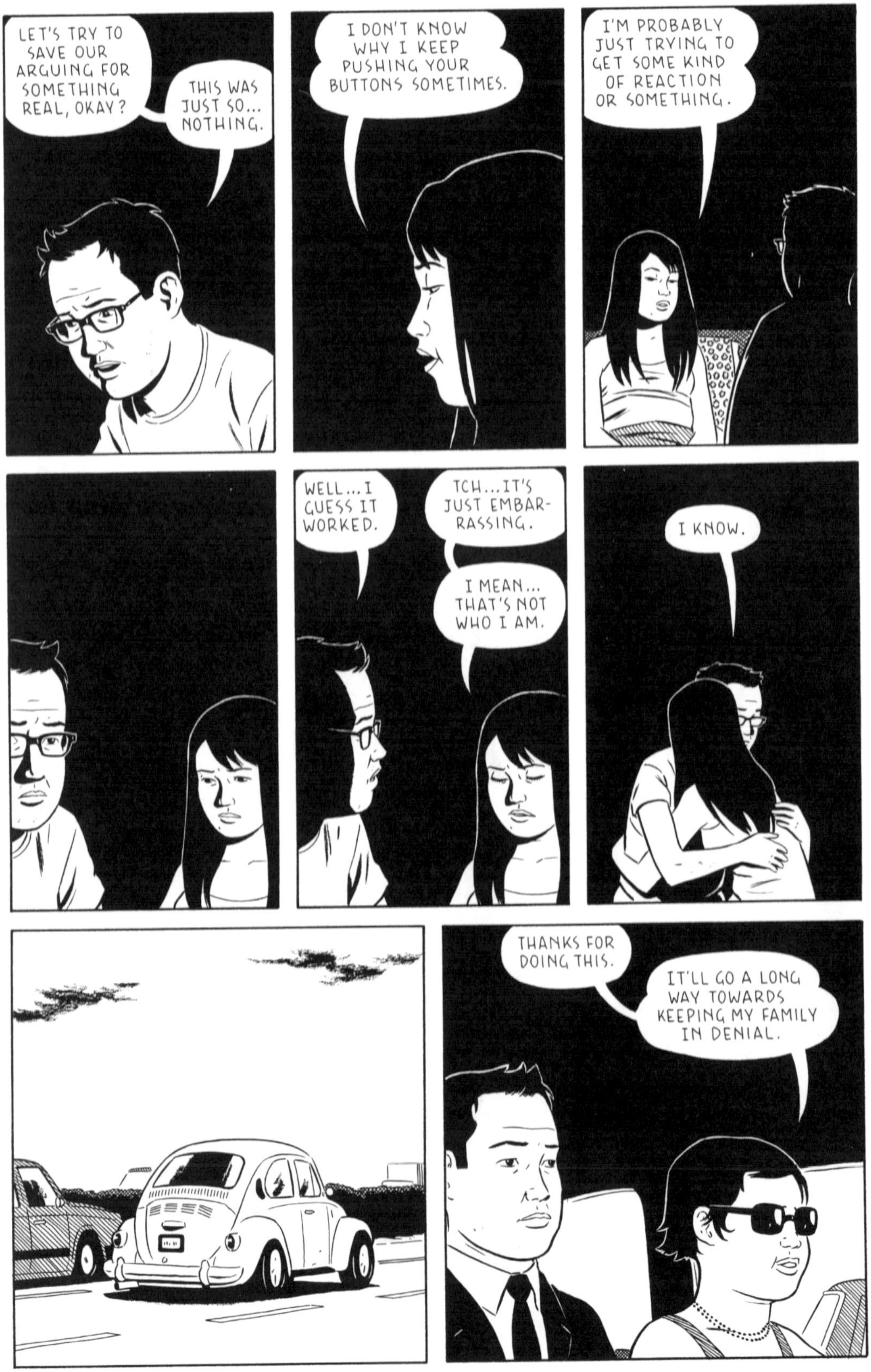

LET'S TRY TO SAVE OUR ARGUING FOR SOMETHING REAL, OKAY?
THIS WAS JUST SO... NOTHING.
I DON'T KNOW WHY I KEEP PUSHING YOUR BUTTONS SOMETIMES.
I'M PROBABLY JUST TRYING TO GET SOME KIND OF REACTION OR SOMETHING.
WELL... I GUESS IT WORKED.
TCH... IT'S JUST EMBARRASSING.
I MEAN... THAT'S NOT WHO I AM.
I KNOW.
THANKS FOR DOING THIS.
IT'LL GO A LONG WAY TOWARDS KEEPING MY FAMILY IN DENIAL.

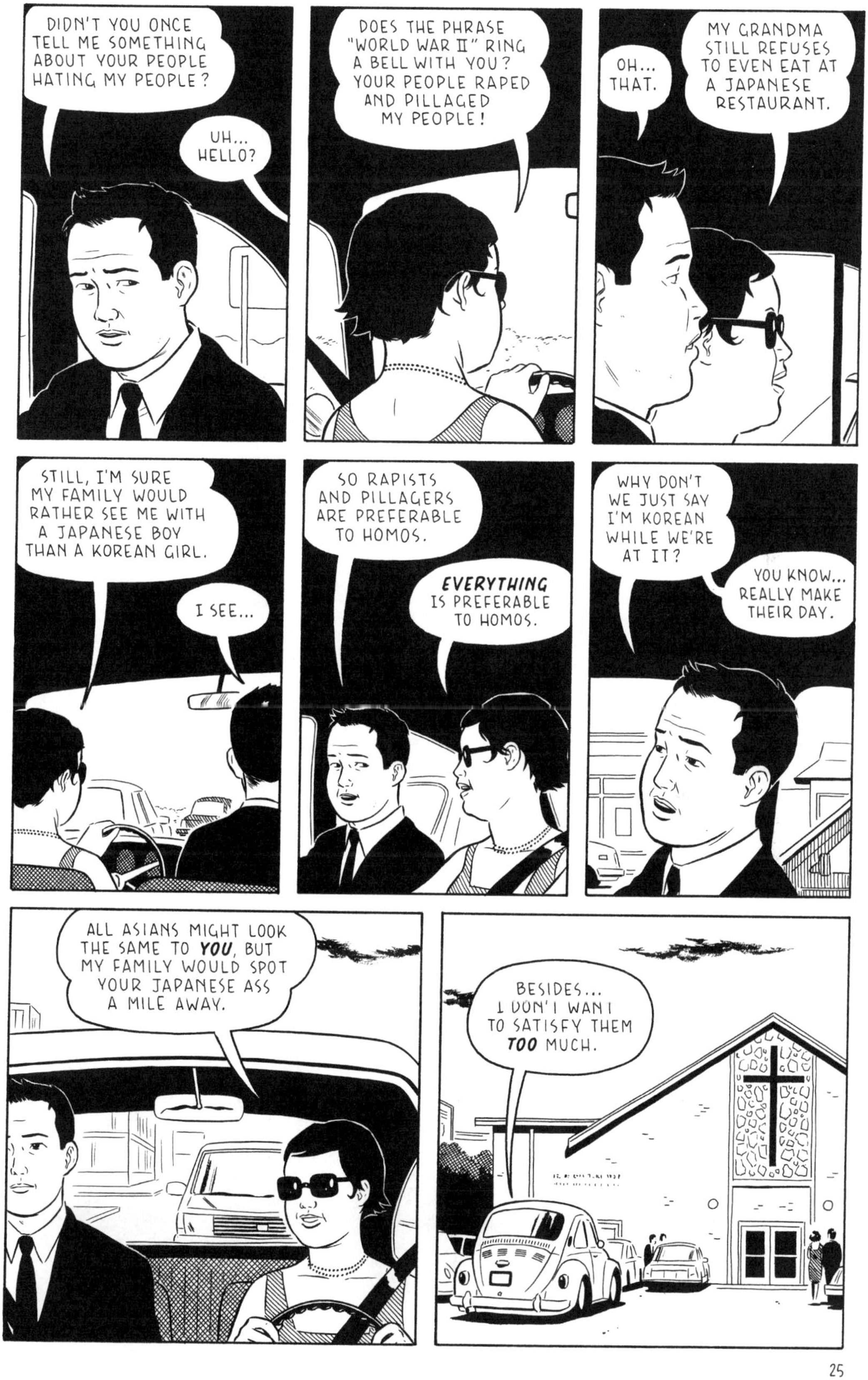
DIDN'T YOU ONCE TELL ME SOMETHING ABOUT YOUR PEOPLE HATING MY PEOPLE?
UH... HELLO?
DOES THE PHRASE "WORLD WAR II" RING A BELL WITH YOU? YOUR PEOPLE RAPED AND PILLAGED MY PEOPLE!
OH... THAT.
MY GRANDMA STILL REFUSES TO EVEN EAT AT A JAPANESE RESTAURANT.
STILL, I'M SURE MY FAMILY WOULD RATHER SEE ME WITH A JAPANESE BOY THAN A KOREAN GIRL.
I SEE...
SO RAPISTS AND PILLAGERS ARE PREFERABLE TO HOMOS.
EVERYTHING IS PREFERABLE TO HOMOS.
WHY DON'T WE JUST SAY I'M KOREAN WHILE WE'RE AT IT?
YOU KNOW... REALLY MAKE THEIR DAY.
ALL ASIANS MIGHT LOOK THE SAME TO YOU, BUT MY FAMILY WOULD SPOT YOUR JAPANESE ASS A MILE AWAY.
BESIDES... I DON'T WANT TO SATISFY THEM TOO MUCH.

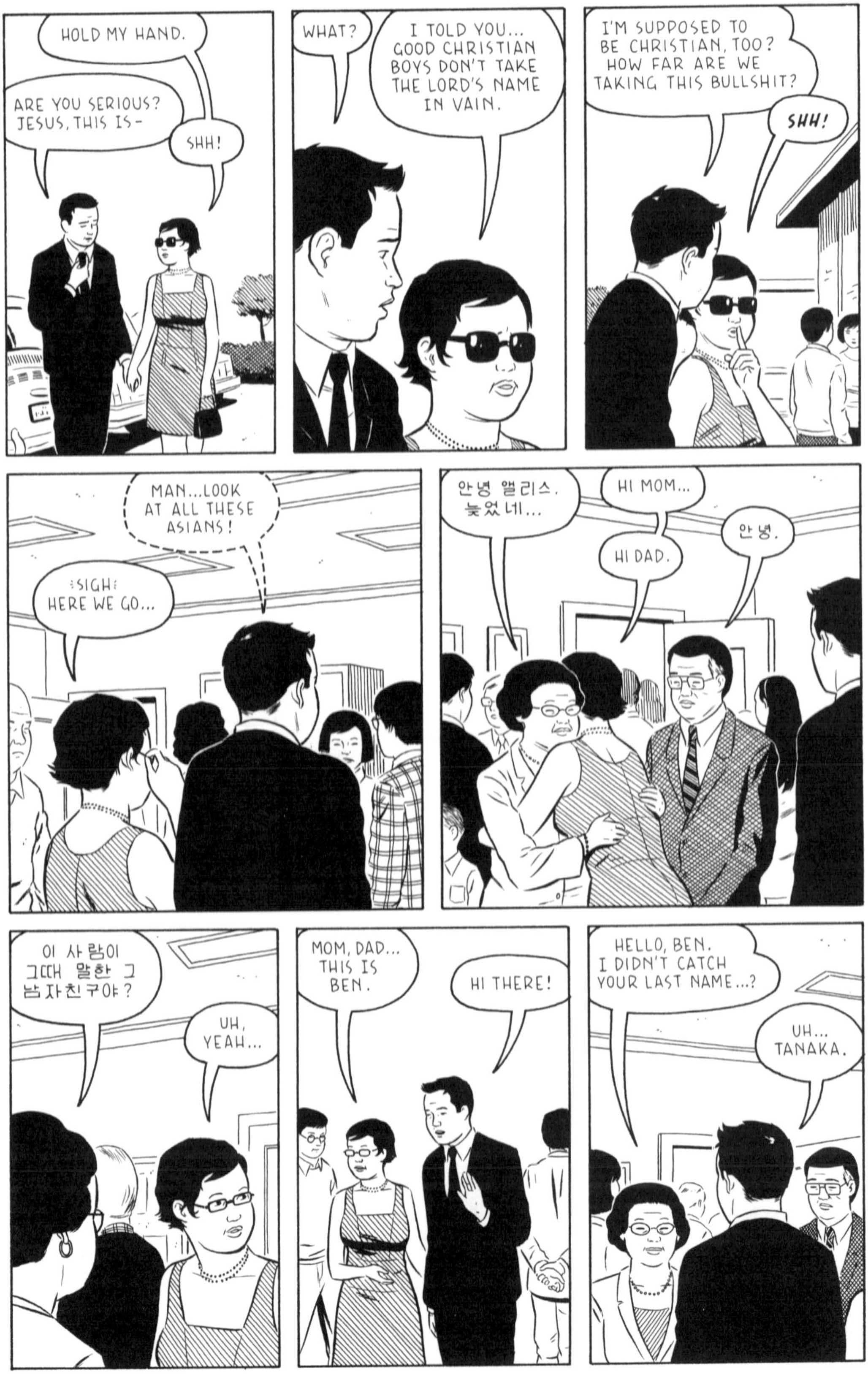
HOLD MY HAND.
ARE YOU SERIOUS? JESUS, THIS IS-
SHH!
WHAT?
I TOLD YOU... GOOD CHRISTIAN BOYS DON'T TAKE THE LORD'S NAME IN VAIN.
I'M SUPPOSED TO BE CHRISTIAN, TOO? HOW FAR ARE WE TAKING THIS BULLSHIT?
SHH!
MAN...LOOK AT ALL THESE ASIANS!
:SIGH: HERE WE GO...
안녕 앨리스. 늦었네...
HI MOM...
HI DAD.
안녕.
이 사람이 그때 말한 그 남자친구야?
UH, YEAH...
MOM, DAD... THIS IS BEN.
HI THERE!
HELLO, BEN. I DIDN'T CATCH YOUR LAST NAME...?
UH... TANAKA.

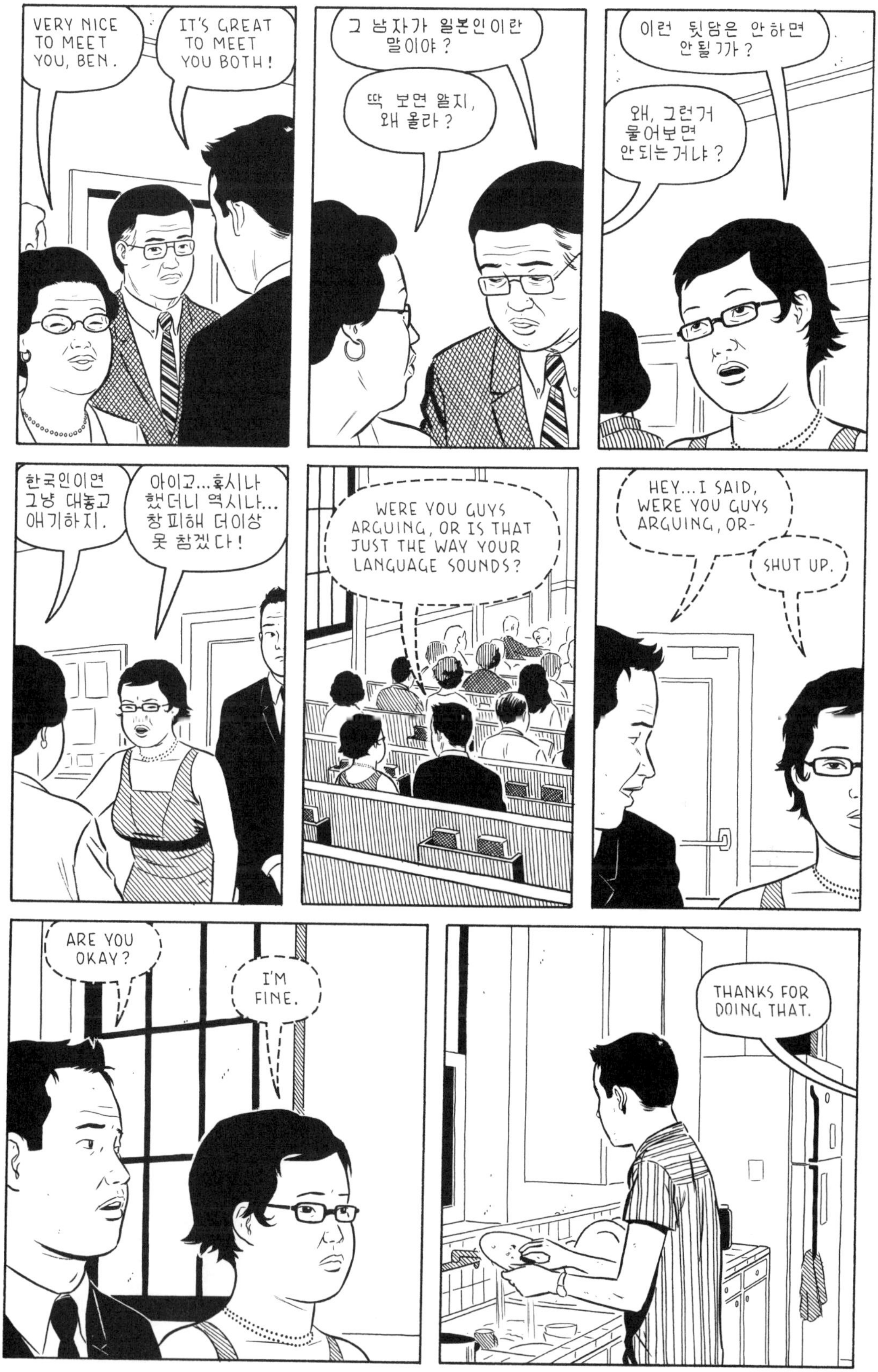
VERY NICE TO MEET YOU, BEN.
IT'S GREAT TO MEET YOU BOTH!
그 남자가 일본인이란 말이야 ?
딱 보면 알지, 왜 올라 ?
이런 뒷담은 안하면 안될까 ?
왜, 그런거 물어보면 안되는거냐 ?
한국인이면 그냥 대놓고 애기하지.
아이고...혹시나 했더니 역시나... 창피해 더이상 못 참겠다 !
WERE YOU GUYS ARGUING, OR IS THAT JUST THE WAY YOUR LANGUAGE SOUNDS?
HEY...I SAID, WERE YOU GUYS ARGUING, OR-
SHUT UP.
ARE YOU OKAY?
I'M FINE.
THANKS FOR DOING THAT.

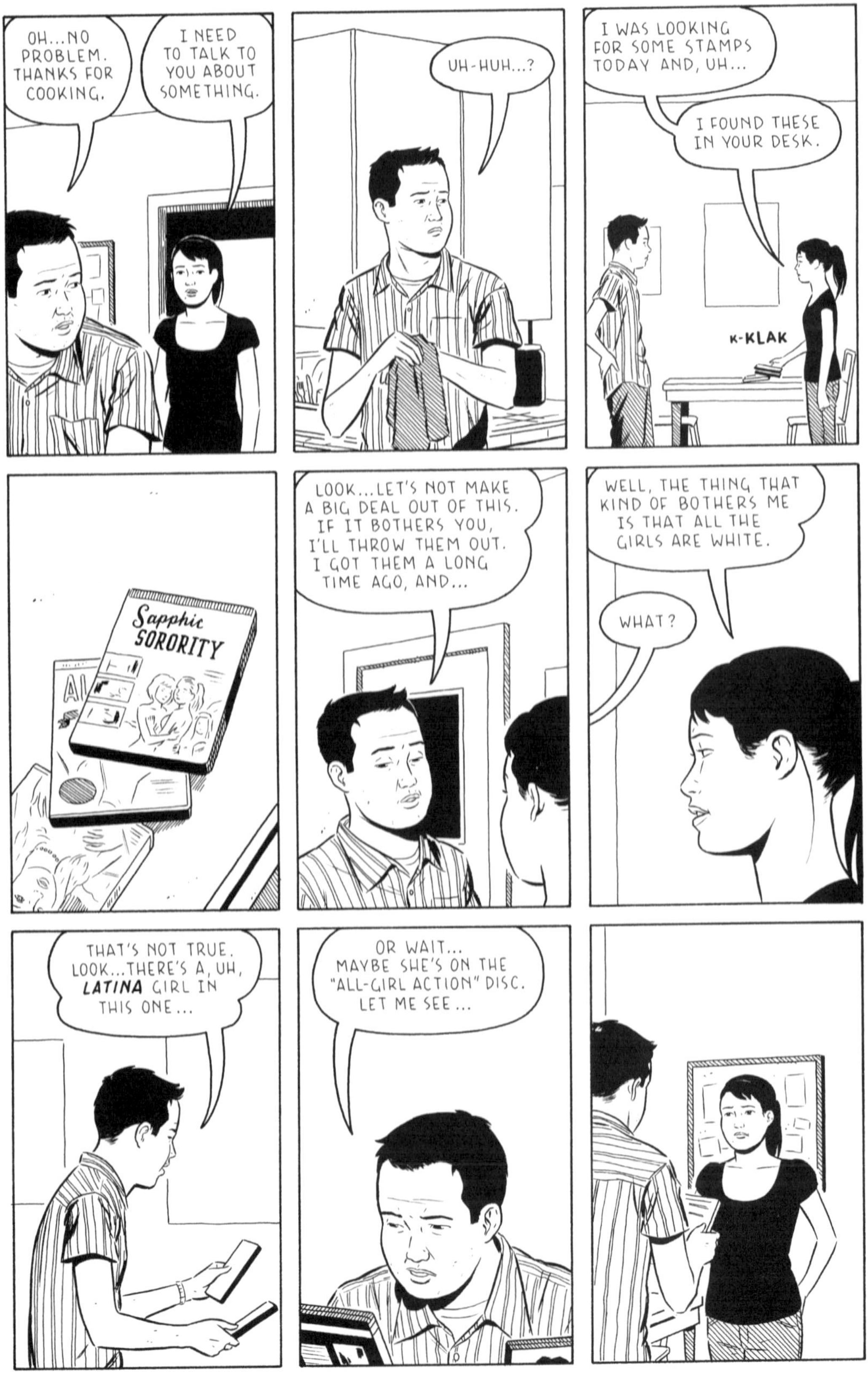
OH...NO PROBLEM. THANKS FOR COOKING.
I NEED TO TALK TO YOU ABOUT SOMETHING.
UH-HUH...?
I WAS LOOKING FOR SOME STAMPS TODAY AND, UH...
I FOUND THESE IN YOUR DESK.
K-KLAK
Sapphic SORORITY
LOOK...LET'S NOT MAKE A BIG DEAL OUT OF THIS. IF IT BOTHERS YOU, I'LL THROW THEM OUT. I GOT THEM A LONG TIME AGO, AND...
WELL, THE THING THAT KIND OF BOTHERS ME IS THAT ALL THE GIRLS ARE WHITE.
WHAT?
THAT'S NOT TRUE. LOOK...THERE'S A, UH, LATINA GIRL IN THIS ONE...
OR WAIT... MAYBE SHE'S ON THE "ALL-GIRL ACTION" DISC. LET ME SEE...

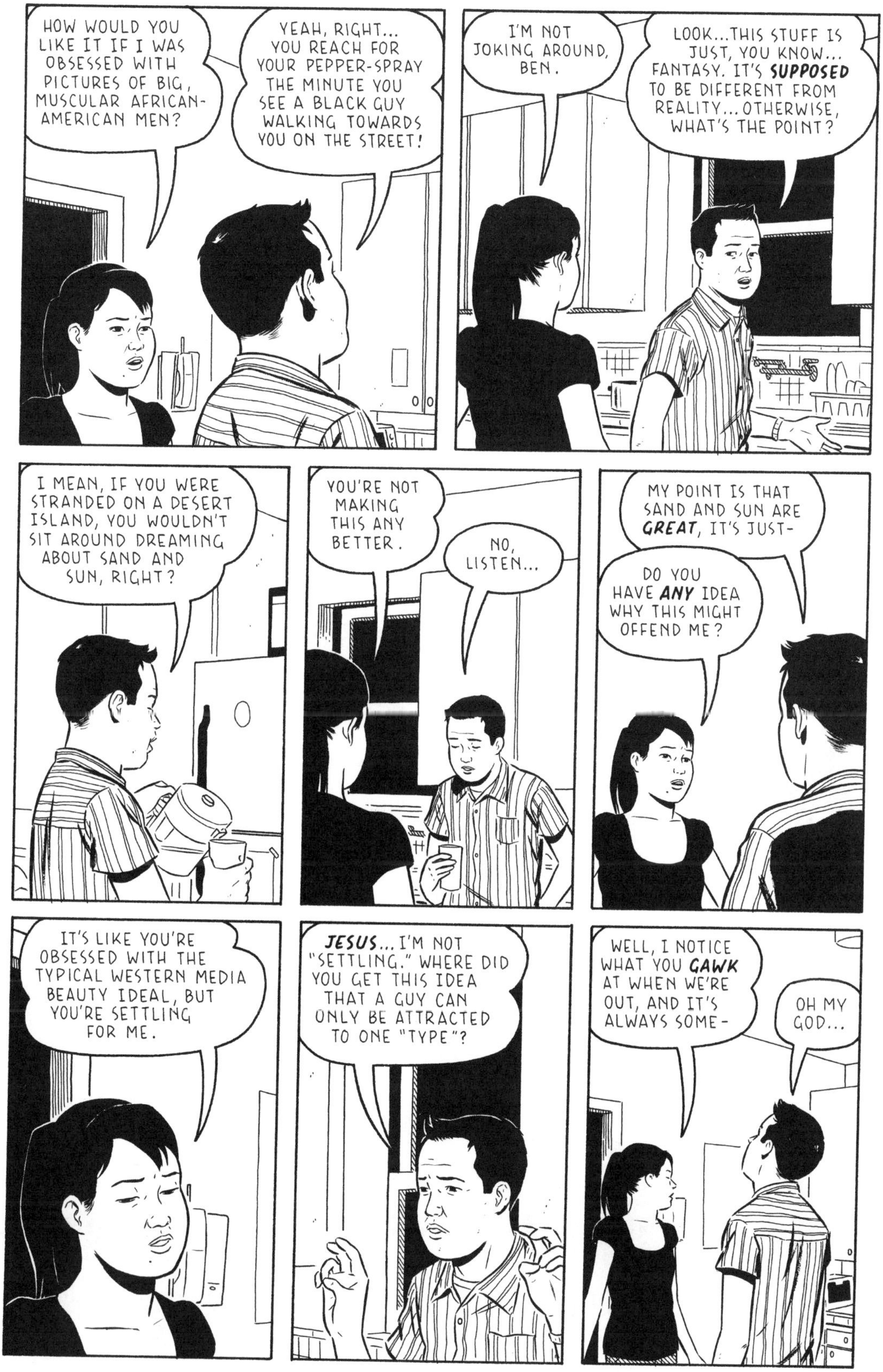
HOW WOULD YOU LIKE IT IF I WAS OBSESSED WITH PICTURES OF BIG, MUSCULAR AFRICAN-AMERICAN MEN?
YEAH, RIGHT... YOU REACH FOR YOUR PEPPER-SPRAY THE MINUTE YOU SEE A BLACK GUY WALKING TOWARDS YOU ON THE STREET!
I'M NOT JOKING AROUND, BEN.
LOOK...THIS STUFF IS JUST, YOU KNOW... FANTASY. IT'S **SUPPOSED** TO BE DIFFERENT FROM REALITY...OTHERWISE, WHAT'S THE POINT?
I MEAN, IF YOU WERE STRANDED ON A DESERT ISLAND, YOU WOULDN'T SIT AROUND DREAMING ABOUT SAND AND SUN, RIGHT?
YOU'RE NOT MAKING THIS ANY BETTER.
NO, LISTEN...
MY POINT IS THAT SAND AND SUN ARE **GREAT**, IT'S JUST-
DO YOU HAVE **ANY** IDEA WHY THIS MIGHT OFFEND ME?
IT'S LIKE YOU'RE OBSESSED WITH THE TYPICAL WESTERN MEDIA BEAUTY IDEAL, BUT YOU'RE SETTLING FOR ME.
JESUS... I'M NOT "SETTLING." WHERE DID YOU GET THIS IDEA THAT A GUY CAN ONLY BE ATTRACTED TO ONE "TYPE"?
WELL, I NOTICE WHAT YOU **GAWK** AT WHEN WE'RE OUT, AND IT'S ALWAYS SOME-
OH MY GOD...

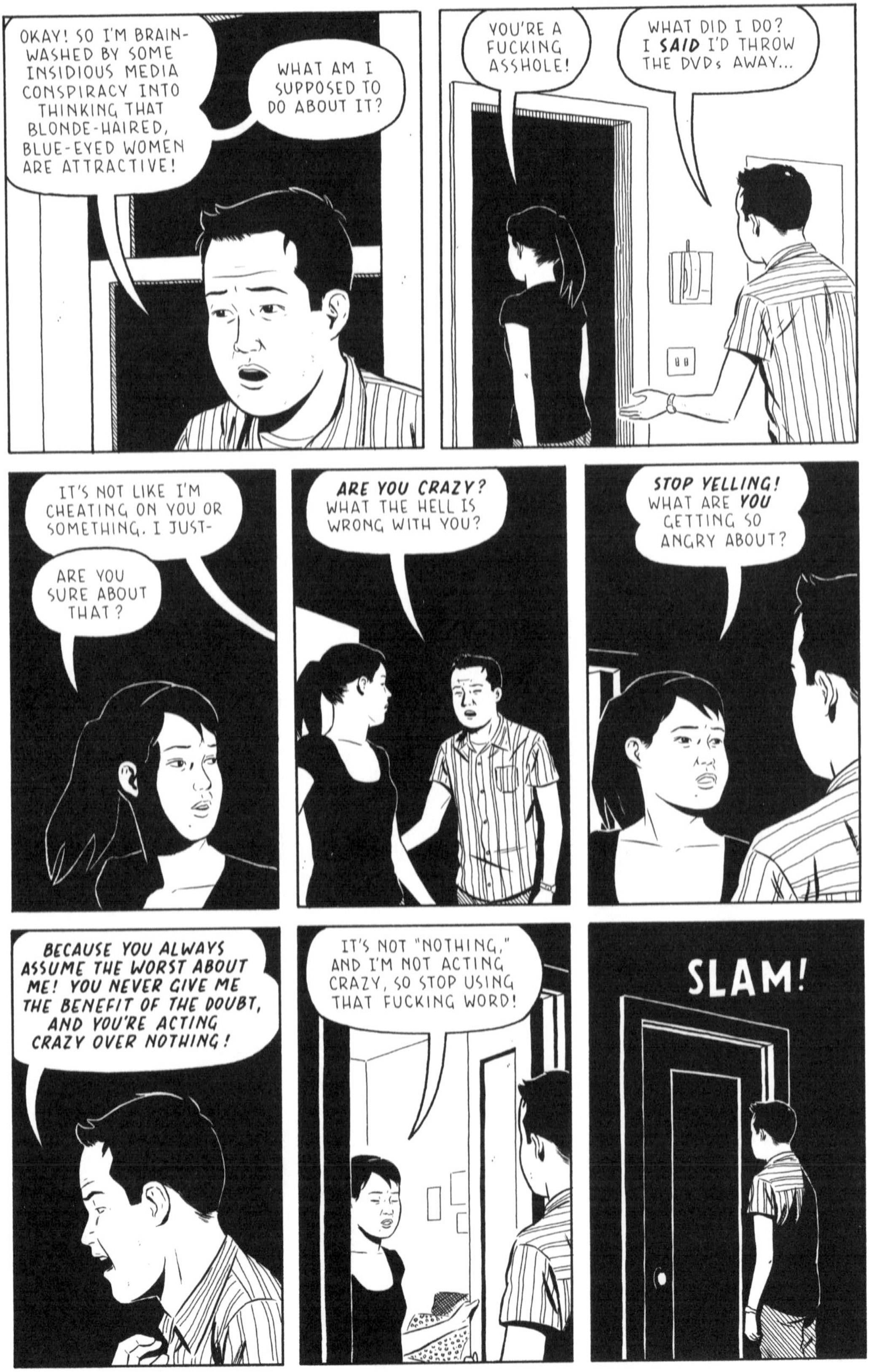

OKAY! SO I'M BRAIN-WASHED BY SOME INSIDIOUS MEDIA CONSPIRACY INTO THINKING THAT BLONDE-HAIRED, BLUE-EYED WOMEN ARE ATTRACTIVE!
WHAT AM I SUPPOSED TO DO ABOUT IT?
YOU'RE A FUCKING ASSHOLE!
WHAT DID I DO? I **SAID** I'D THROW THE DVDs AWAY...
IT'S NOT LIKE I'M CHEATING ON YOU OR SOMETHING. I JUST-
ARE YOU SURE ABOUT THAT?
ARE YOU CRAZY? WHAT THE HELL IS WRONG WITH YOU?
STOP YELLING! WHAT ARE **YOU** GETTING SO ANGRY ABOUT?
BECAUSE YOU ALWAYS ASSUME THE WORST ABOUT ME! YOU NEVER GIVE ME THE BENEFIT OF THE DOUBT, AND YOU'RE ACTING CRAZY OVER NOTHING!
IT'S NOT "NOTHING," AND I'M NOT ACTING CRAZY, SO STOP USING THAT FUCKING WORD!
SLAM!

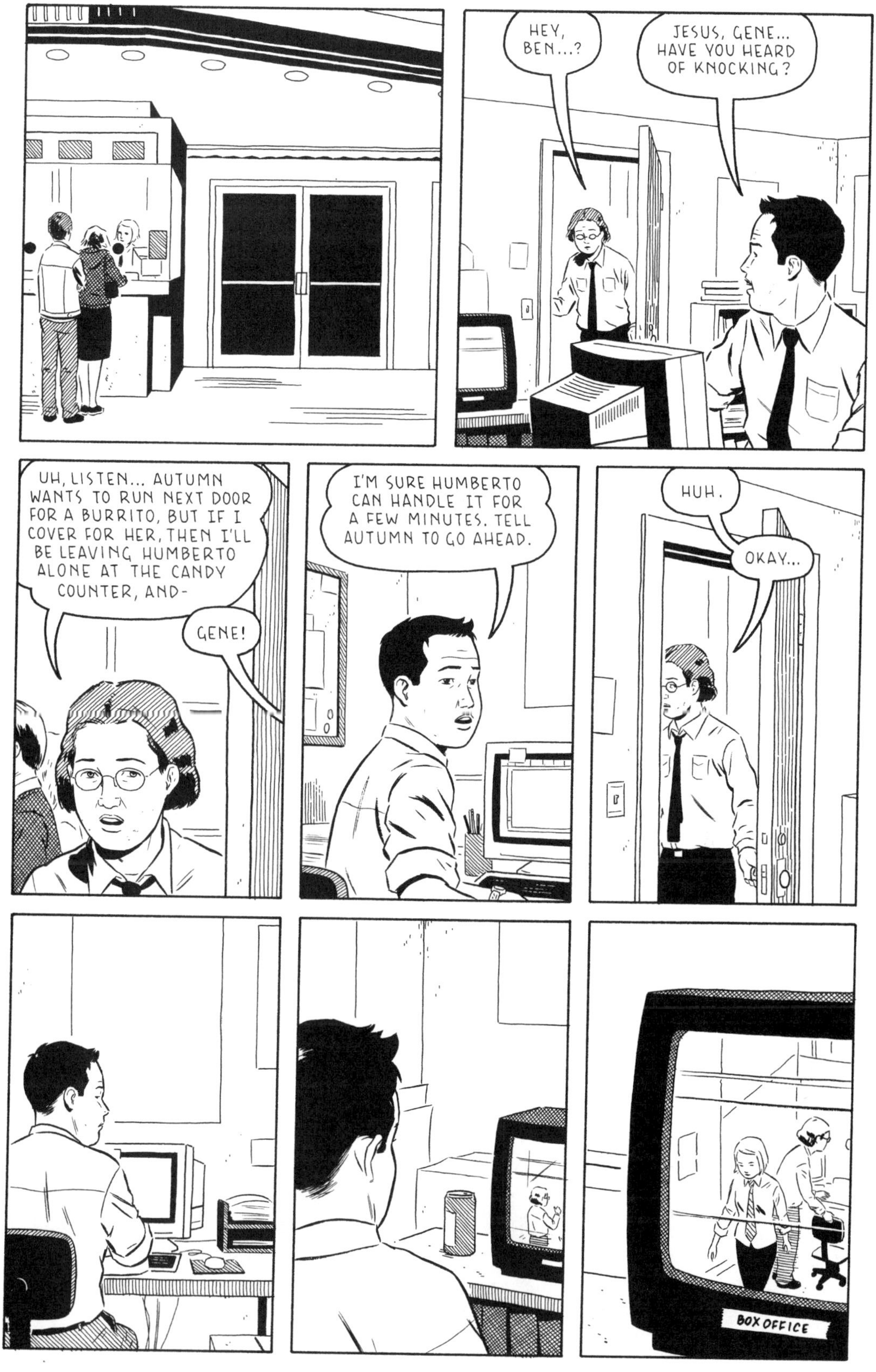
HEY, BEN...?
JESUS, GENE... HAVE YOU HEARD OF KNOCKING?
UH, LISTEN... AUTUMN WANTS TO RUN NEXT DOOR FOR A BURRITO, BUT IF I COVER FOR HER, THEN I'LL BE LEAVING HUMBERTO ALONE AT THE CANDY COUNTER, AND-
GENE!
I'M SURE HUMBERTO CAN HANDLE IT FOR A FEW MINUTES. TELL AUTUMN TO GO AHEAD.
HUH.
OKAY...
BOX OFFICE

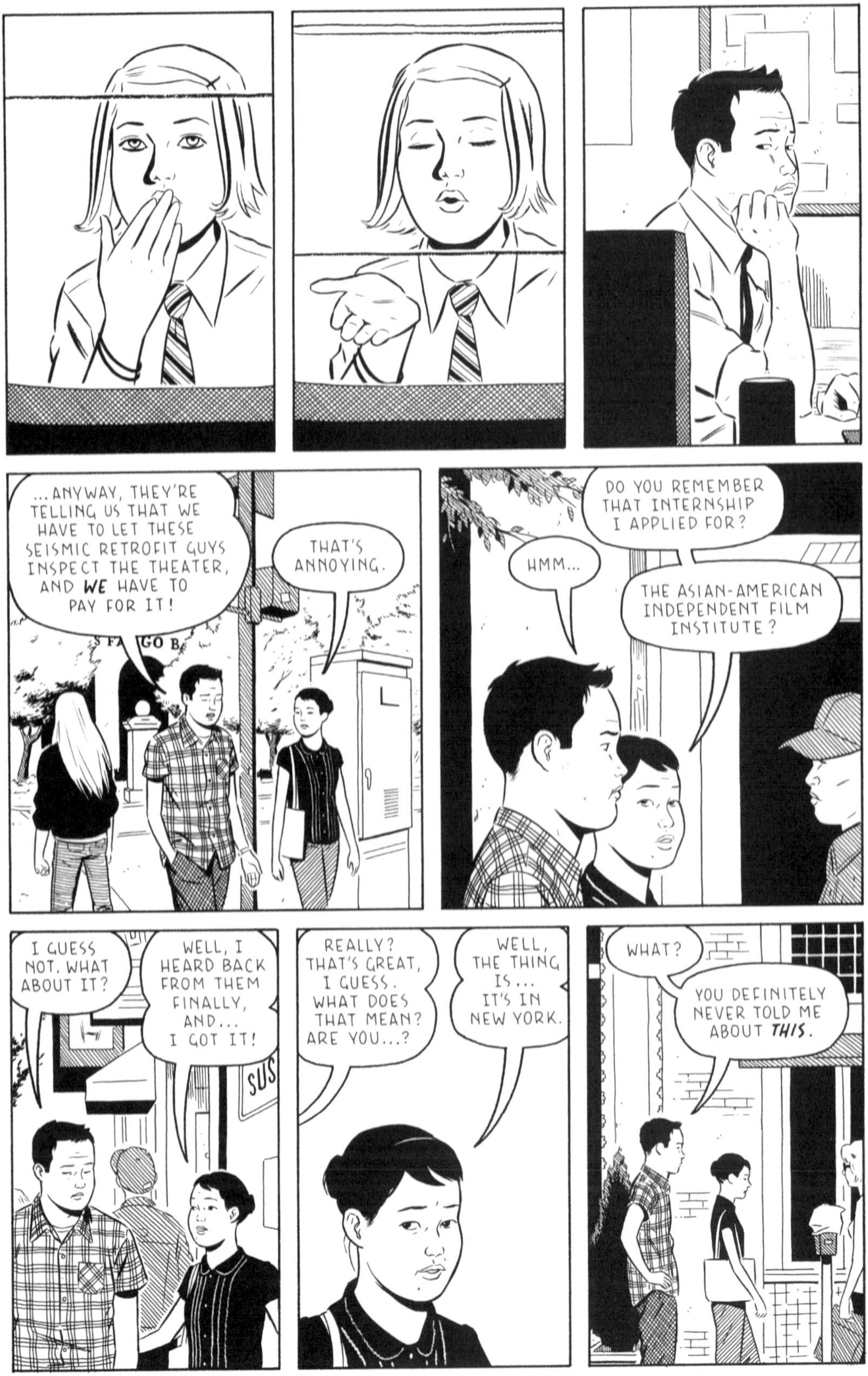

...ANYWAY, THEY'RE TELLING US THAT WE HAVE TO LET THESE SEISMIC RETROFIT GUYS INSPECT THE THEATER, AND **WE** HAVE TO PAY FOR IT!
THAT'S ANNOYING.
DO YOU REMEMBER THAT INTERNSHIP I APPLIED FOR?
HMM...
THE ASIAN-AMERICAN INDEPENDENT FILM INSTITUTE?
I GUESS NOT. WHAT ABOUT IT?
WELL, I HEARD BACK FROM THEM FINALLY, AND... I GOT IT!
REALLY? THAT'S GREAT, I GUESS. WHAT DOES THAT MEAN? ARE YOU...?
WELL, THE THING IS... IT'S IN NEW YORK.
WHAT?
YOU DEFINITELY NEVER TOLD ME ABOUT **THIS**.

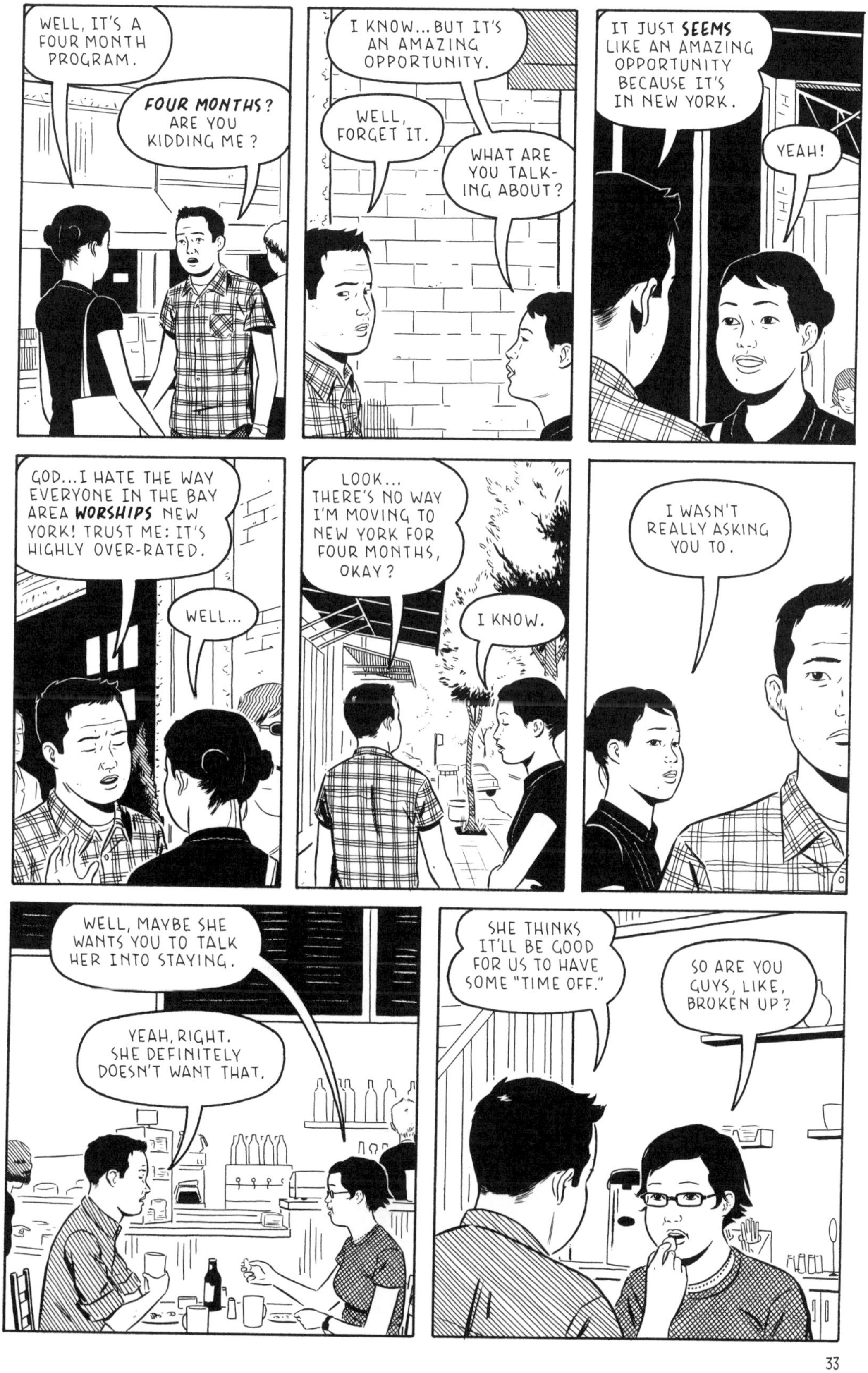
WELL, IT'S A FOUR MONTH PROGRAM.
FOUR MONTHS? ARE YOU KIDDING ME?
I KNOW...BUT IT'S AN AMAZING OPPORTUNITY.
WELL, FORGET IT.
WHAT ARE YOU TALKING ABOUT?
IT JUST SEEMS LIKE AN AMAZING OPPORTUNITY BECAUSE IT'S IN NEW YORK.
YEAH!
GOD...I HATE THE WAY EVERYONE IN THE BAY AREA WORSHIPS NEW YORK! TRUST ME: IT'S HIGHLY OVER-RATED.
WELL...
LOOK... THERE'S NO WAY I'M MOVING TO NEW YORK FOR FOUR MONTHS, OKAY?
I KNOW.
I WASN'T REALLY ASKING YOU TO.
WELL, MAYBE SHE WANTS YOU TO TALK HER INTO STAYING.
YEAH, RIGHT. SHE DEFINITELY DOESN'T WANT THAT.
SHE THINKS IT'LL BE GOOD FOR US TO HAVE SOME "TIME OFF."
SO ARE YOU GUYS, LIKE, BROKEN UP?

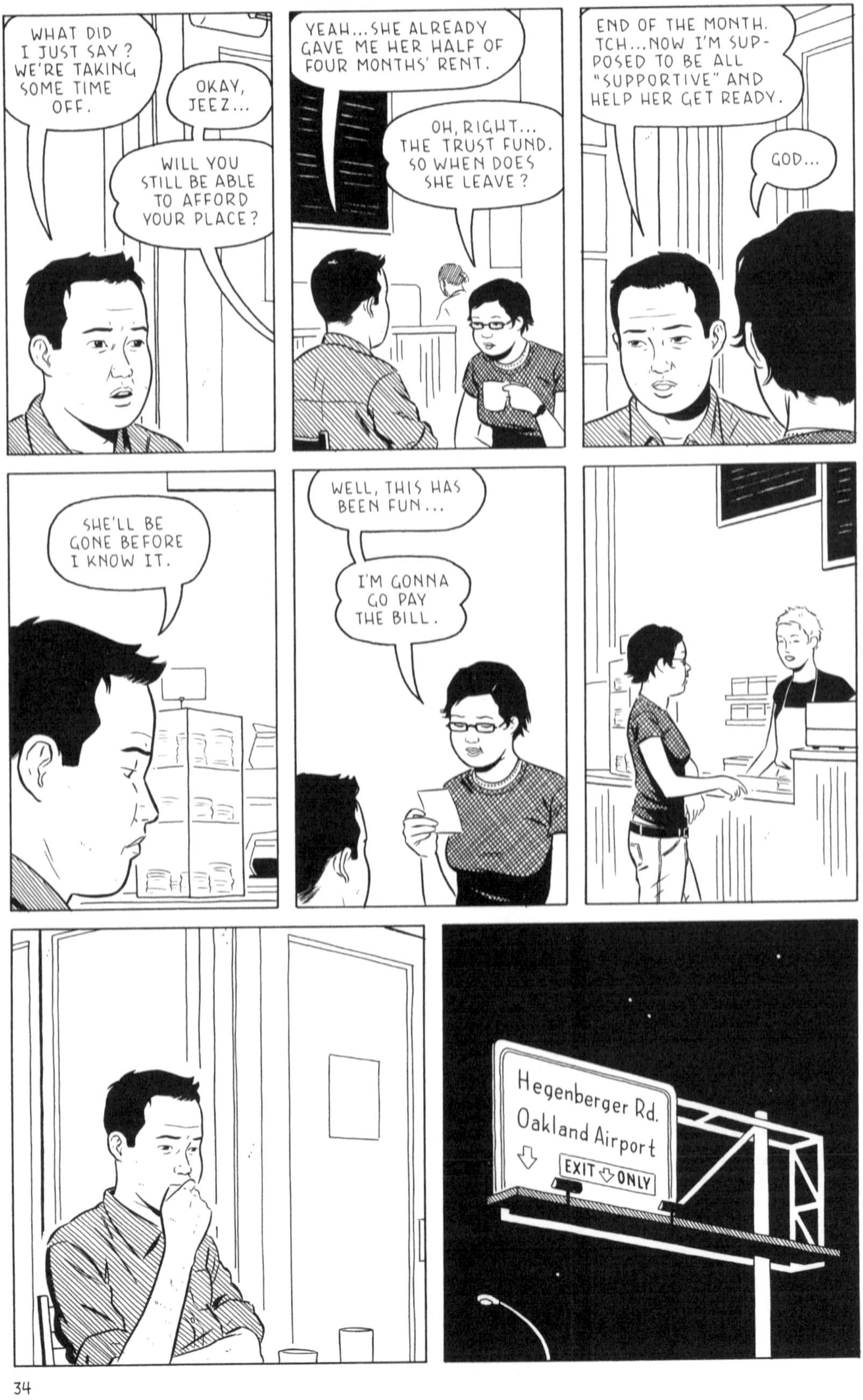
WHAT DID I JUST SAY? WE'RE TAKING SOME TIME OFF.
OKAY, JEEZ...
WILL YOU STILL BE ABLE TO AFFORD YOUR PLACE?
YEAH...SHE ALREADY GAVE ME HER HALF OF FOUR MONTHS' RENT.
OH, RIGHT... THE TRUST FUND. SO WHEN DOES SHE LEAVE?
END OF THE MONTH. TCH...NOW I'M SUPPOSED TO BE ALL "SUPPORTIVE" AND HELP HER GET READY.
GOD...
SHE'LL BE GONE BEFORE I KNOW IT.
WELL, THIS HAS BEEN FUN...
I'M GONNA GO PAY THE BILL.
Hegenberger Rd.
Oakland Airport
EXIT ONLY

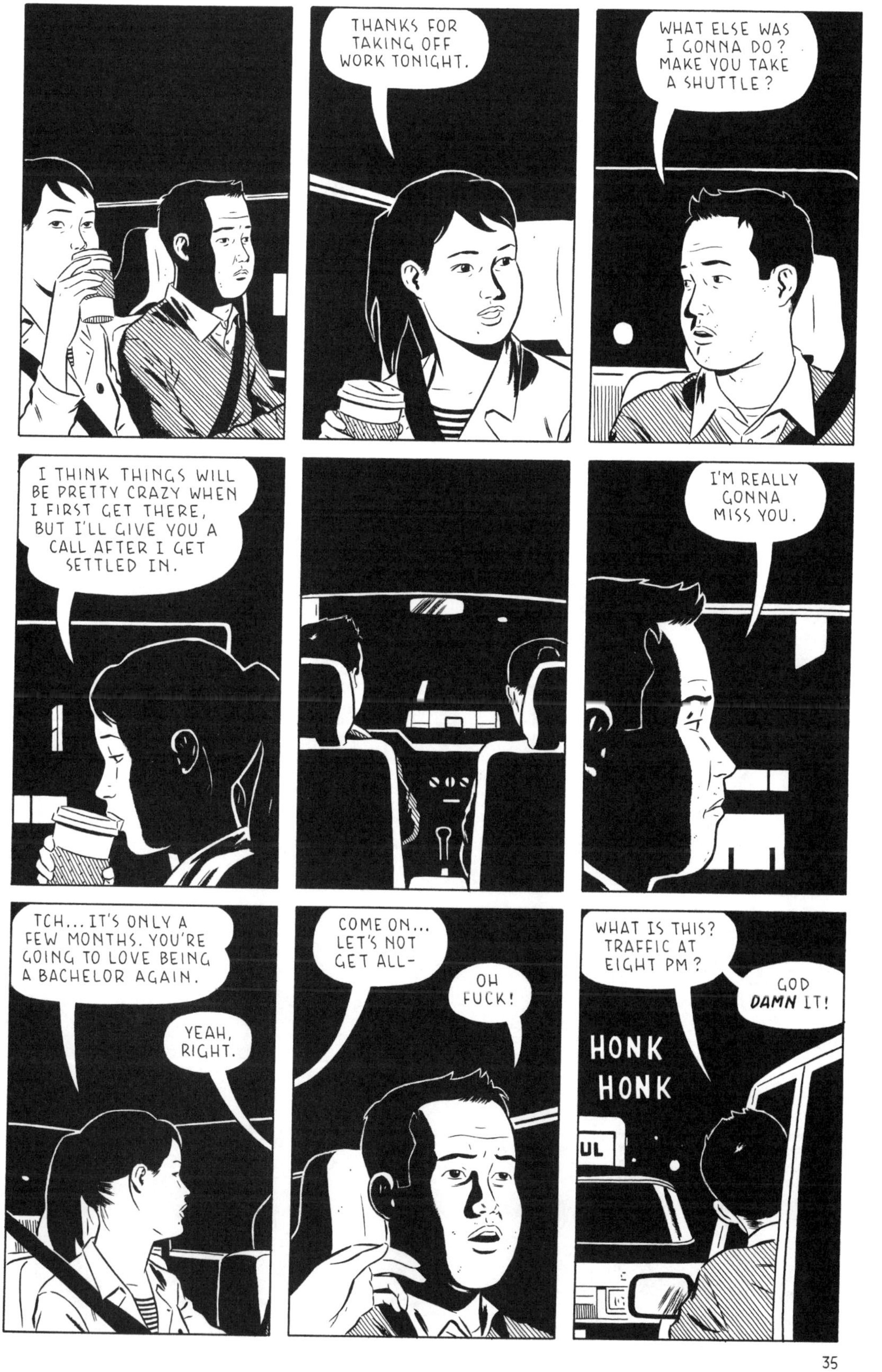
THANKS FOR TAKING OFF WORK TONIGHT.
WHAT ELSE WAS I GONNA DO? MAKE YOU TAKE A SHUTTLE?
I THINK THINGS WILL BE PRETTY CRAZY WHEN I FIRST GET THERE, BUT I'LL GIVE YOU A CALL AFTER I GET SETTLED IN.
I'M REALLY GONNA MISS YOU.
TCH... IT'S ONLY A FEW MONTHS. YOU'RE GOING TO LOVE BEING A BACHELOR AGAIN.
YEAH, RIGHT.
COME ON... LET'S NOT GET ALL-
OH FUCK!
WHAT IS THIS? TRAFFIC AT EIGHT PM?
GOD **DAMN** IT!
HONK
HONK
UL

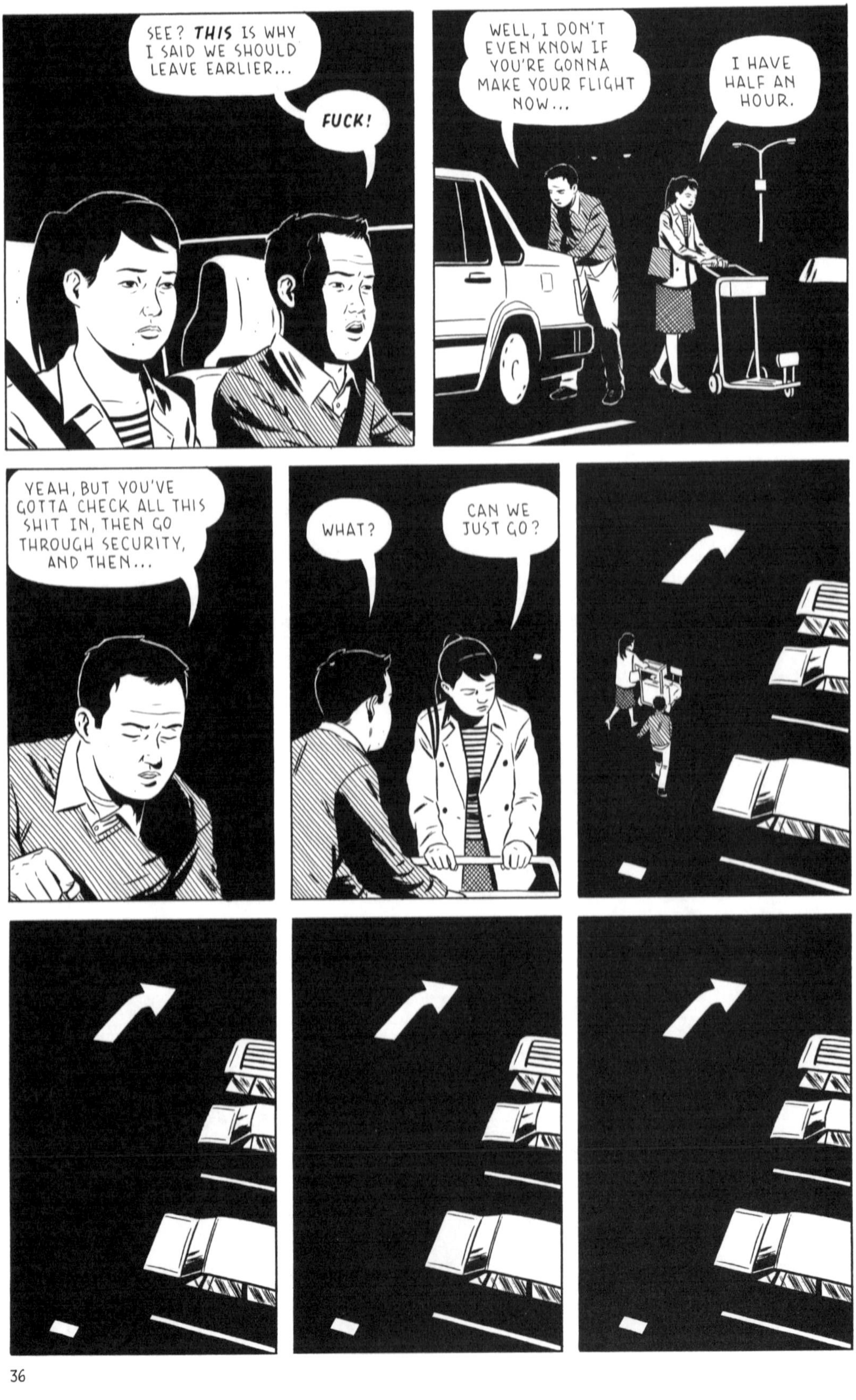
SEE? **THIS** IS WHY I SAID WE SHOULD LEAVE EARLIER...
FUCK!
WELL, I DON'T EVEN KNOW IF YOU'RE GONNA MAKE YOUR FLIGHT NOW...
I HAVE HALF AN HOUR.
YEAH, BUT YOU'VE GOTTA CHECK ALL THIS SHIT IN, THEN GO THROUGH SECURITY, AND THEN...
WHAT?
CAN WE JUST GO?

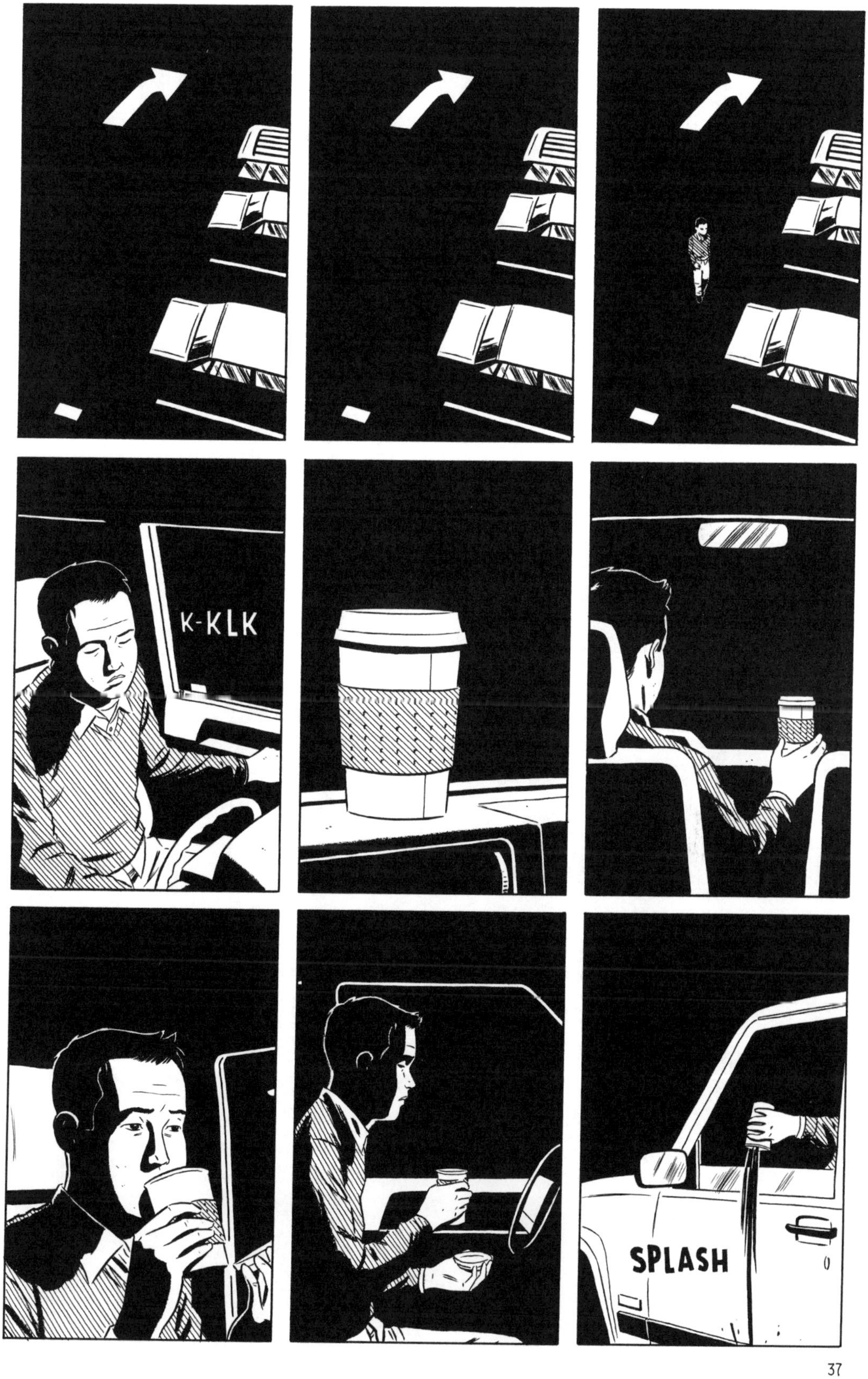
K-KLK
SPLASH

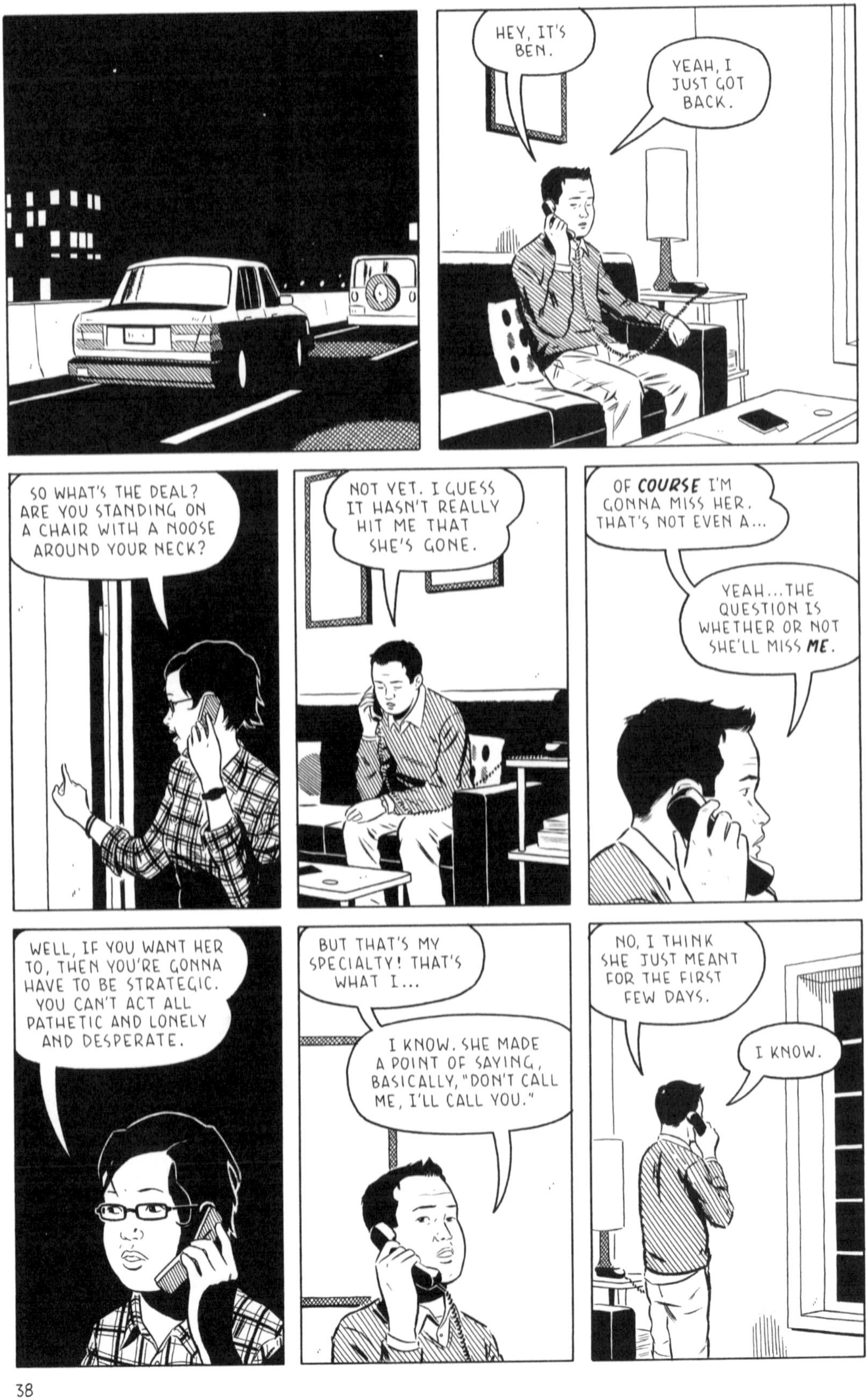
HEY, IT'S BEN.
YEAH, I JUST GOT BACK.
SO WHAT'S THE DEAL? ARE YOU STANDING ON A CHAIR WITH A NOOSE AROUND YOUR NECK?
NOT YET. I GUESS IT HASN'T REALLY HIT ME THAT SHE'S GONE.
OF **COURSE** I'M GONNA MISS HER. THAT'S NOT EVEN A...
YEAH...THE QUESTION IS WHETHER OR NOT SHE'LL MISS **ME**.
WELL, IF YOU WANT HER TO, THEN YOU'RE GONNA HAVE TO BE STRATEGIC. YOU CAN'T ACT ALL PATHETIC AND LONELY AND DESPERATE.
BUT THAT'S MY SPECIALTY! THAT'S WHAT I...
I KNOW. SHE MADE A POINT OF SAYING, BASICALLY, "DON'T CALL ME, I'LL CALL YOU."
NO, I THINK SHE JUST MEANT FOR THE FIRST FEW DAYS.
I KNOW.

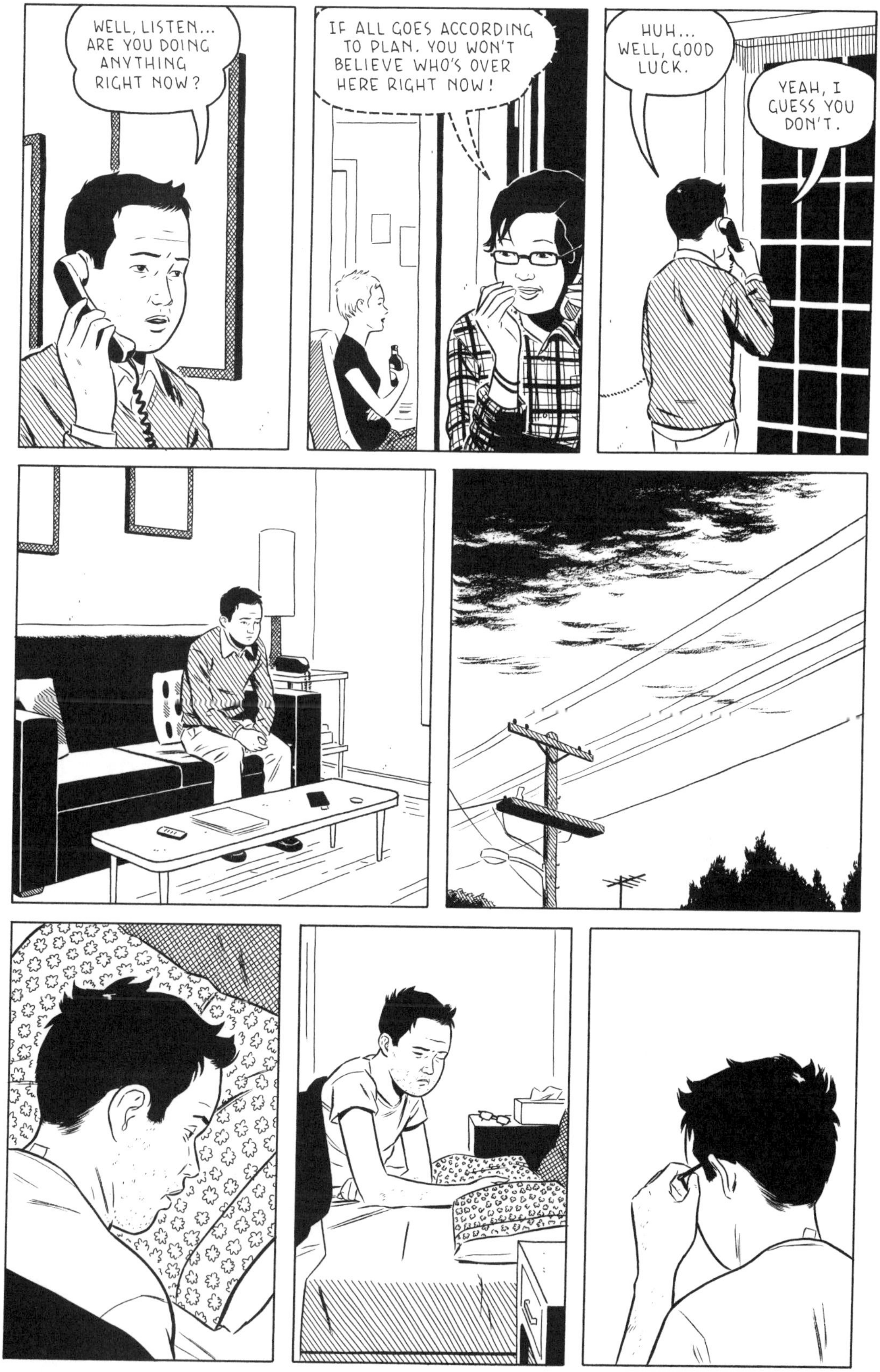
WELL, LISTEN... ARE YOU DOING ANYTHING RIGHT NOW?
IF ALL GOES ACCORDING TO PLAN. YOU WON'T BELIEVE WHO'S OVER HERE RIGHT NOW!
HUH... WELL, GOOD LUCK.
YEAH, I GUESS YOU DON'T.

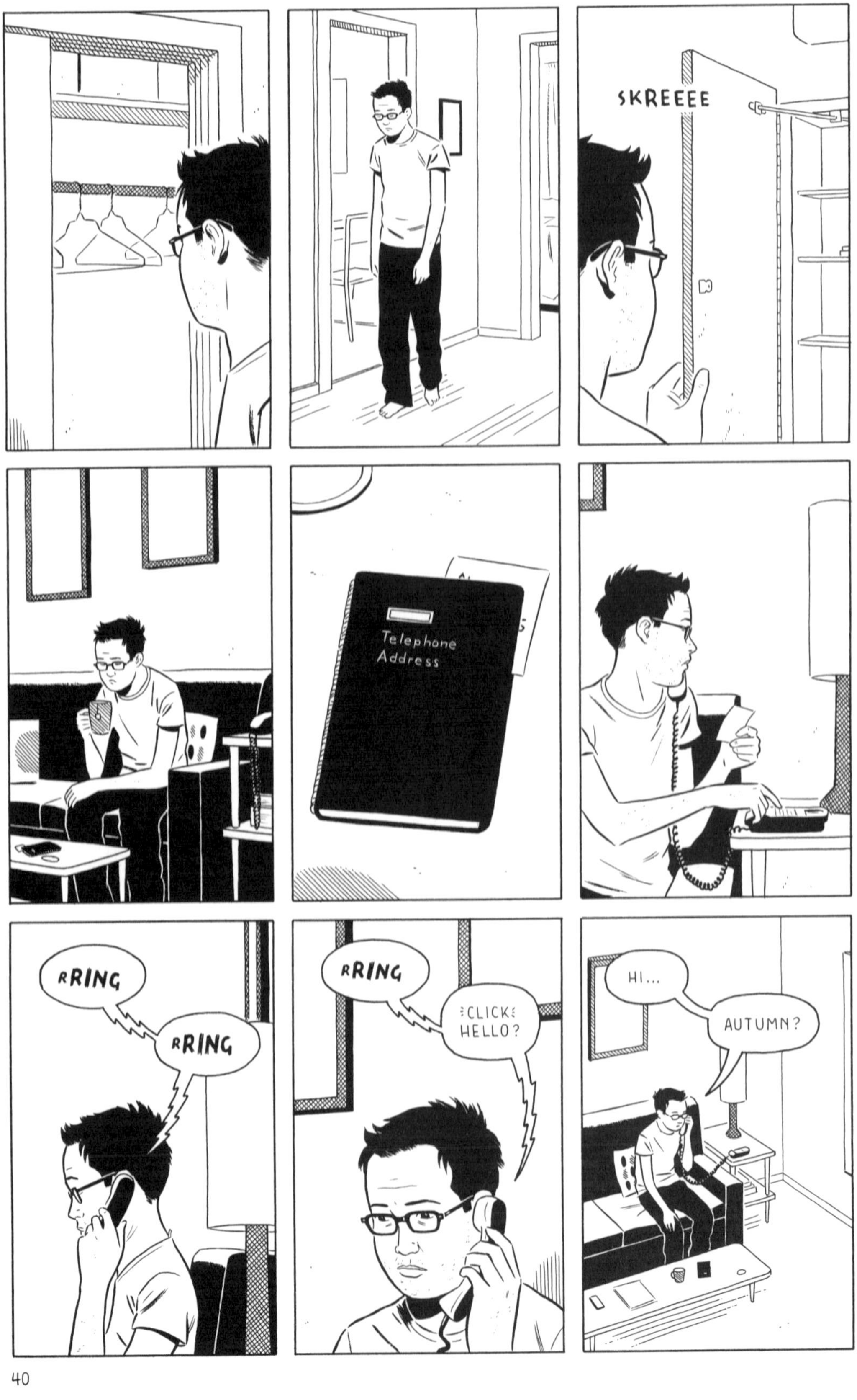
SKREEEE
Telephone
Address
RRING
RRING
RRING
CLICK
HELLO?
HI...
AUTUMN?

CHAPTER TWO

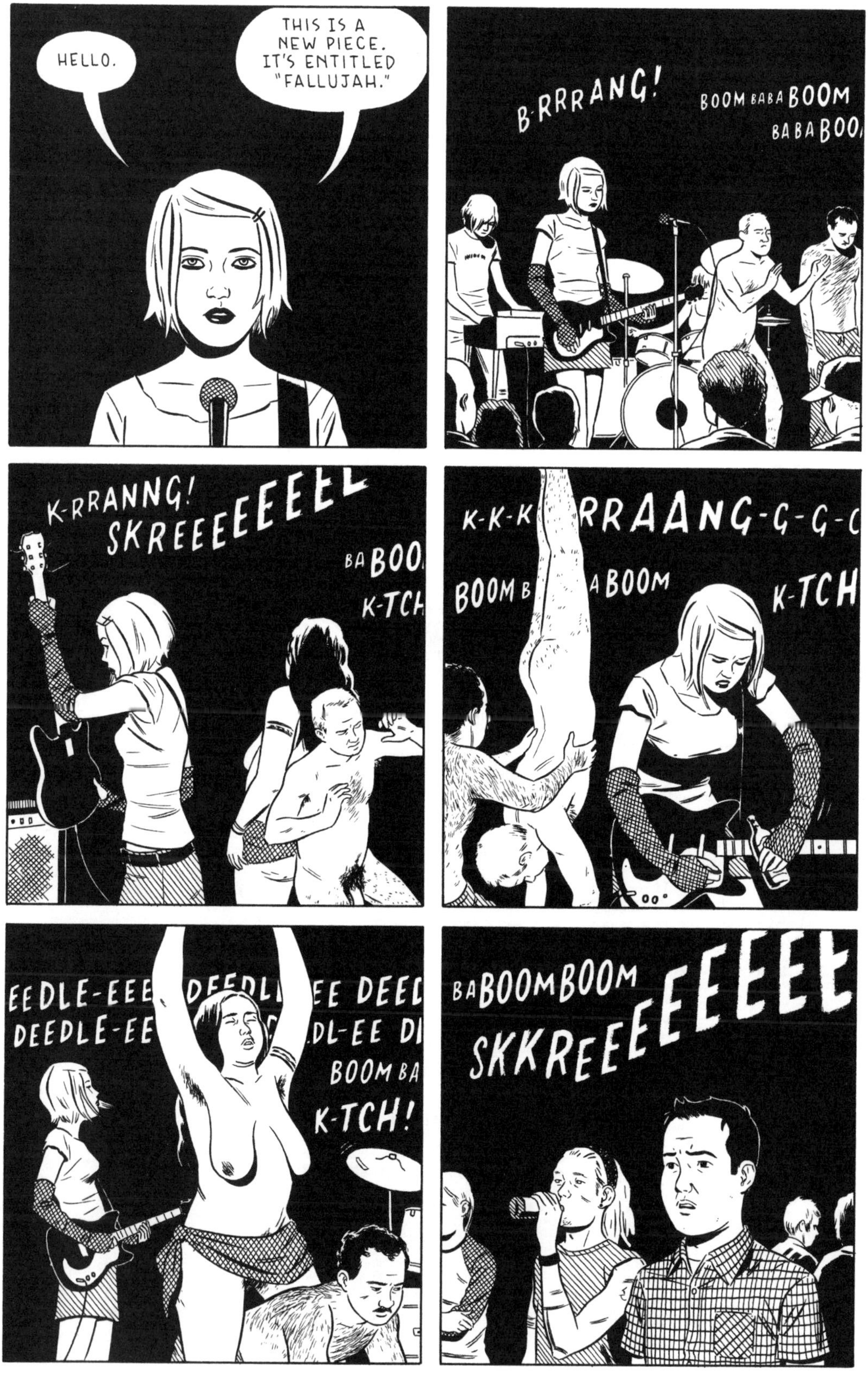
HELLO.
THIS IS A NEW PIECE. IT'S ENTITLED "FALLUJAH."
B-RRRANG!
BOOM BABA BOOM
BA BA BOO
K-RRANNG!
SKREEEEEEEL
BA BOO
K-TCH
K-K-K RRAANG-G-G-G
BOOM B A BOOM
K-TCH
EEDLE-EEE DEEDL EE DEED
DEEDLE-EE DL-EE D
BOOM BA
K-TCH!
BA BOOM BOOM
SKKREEEEEEEL

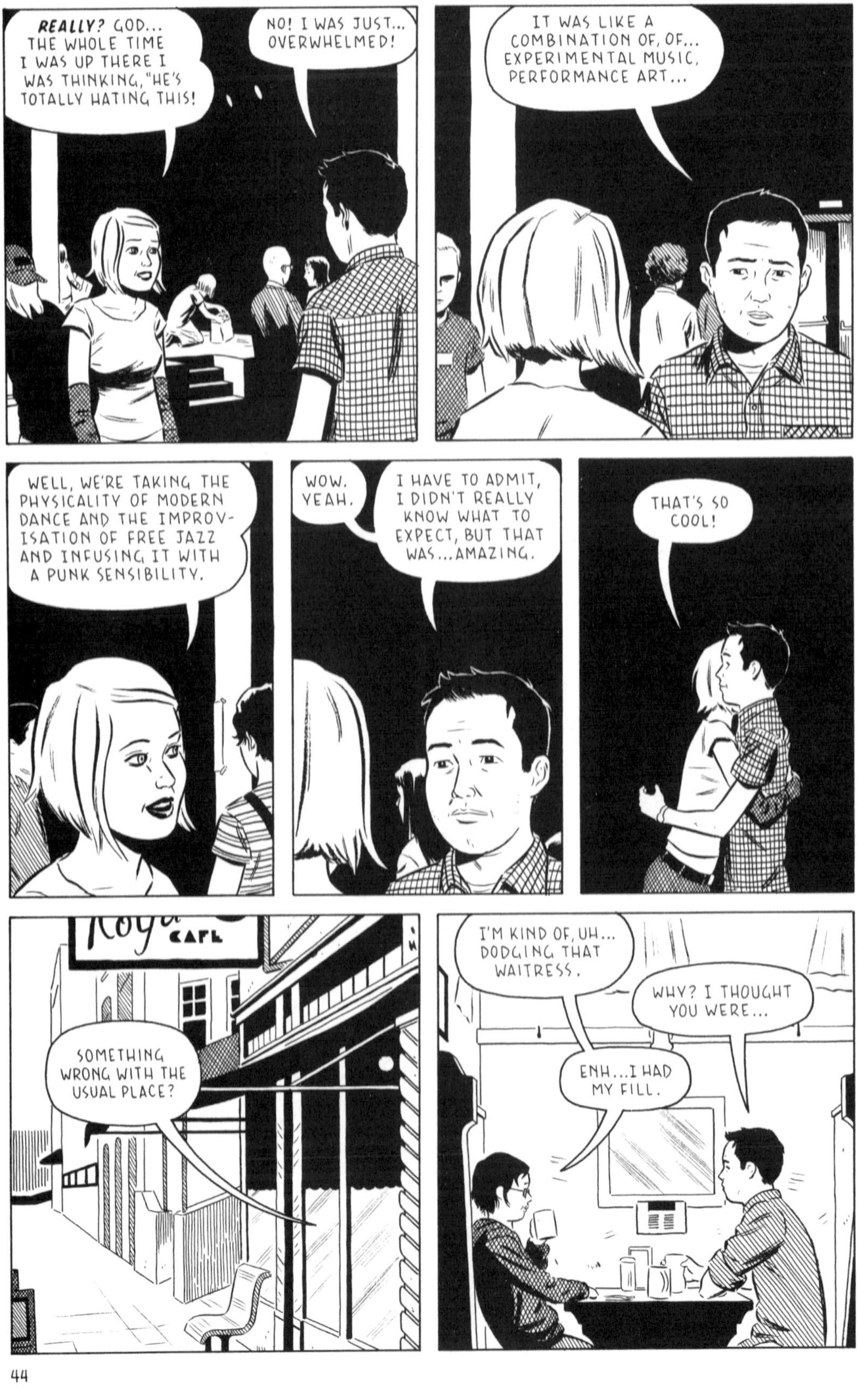
REALLY? GOD... THE WHOLE TIME I WAS UP THERE I WAS THINKING, "HE'S TOTALLY HATING THIS!
NO! I WAS JUST... OVERWHELMED!
IT WAS LIKE A COMBINATION OF, OF... EXPERIMENTAL MUSIC, PERFORMANCE ART...
WELL, WE'RE TAKING THE PHYSICALITY OF MODERN DANCE AND THE IMPROVISATION OF FREE JAZZ AND INFUSING IT WITH A PUNK SENSIBILITY.
WOW. YEAH.
I HAVE TO ADMIT, I DIDN'T REALLY KNOW WHAT TO EXPECT, BUT THAT WAS... AMAZING.
THAT'S SO COOL!
CAFE
SOMETHING WRONG WITH THE USUAL PLACE?
I'M KIND OF, UH... DODGING THAT WAITRESS.
WHY? I THOUGHT YOU WERE...
ENH... I HAD MY FILL.

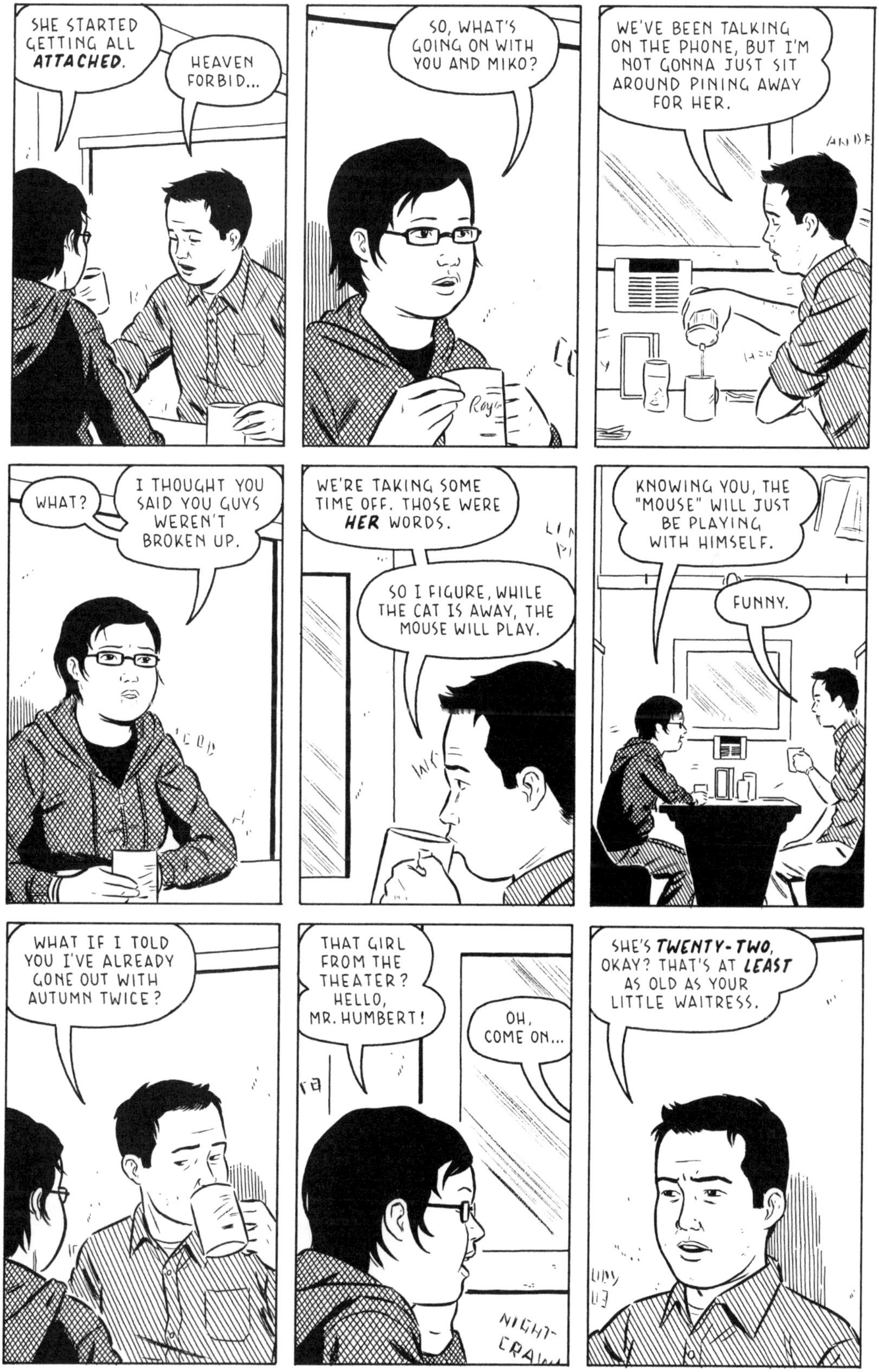
SHE STARTED GETTING ALL **ATTACHED.**
HEAVEN FORBID...
SO, WHAT'S GOING ON WITH YOU AND MIKO?
WE'VE BEEN TALKING ON THE PHONE, BUT I'M NOT GONNA JUST SIT AROUND PINING AWAY FOR HER.
WHAT?
I THOUGHT YOU SAID YOU GUYS WEREN'T BROKEN UP.
WE'RE TAKING SOME TIME OFF. THOSE WERE **HER** WORDS.
SO I FIGURE, WHILE THE CAT IS AWAY, THE MOUSE WILL PLAY.
KNOWING YOU, THE "MOUSE" WILL JUST BE PLAYING WITH HIMSELF.
FUNNY.
WHAT IF I TOLD YOU I'VE ALREADY GONE OUT WITH AUTUMN TWICE?
THAT GIRL FROM THE THEATER? HELLO, MR. HUMBERT!
OH, COME ON...
SHE'S **TWENTY-TWO**, OKAY? THAT'S AT **LEAST** AS OLD AS YOUR LITTLE WAITRESS.
NIGHT-CRAW

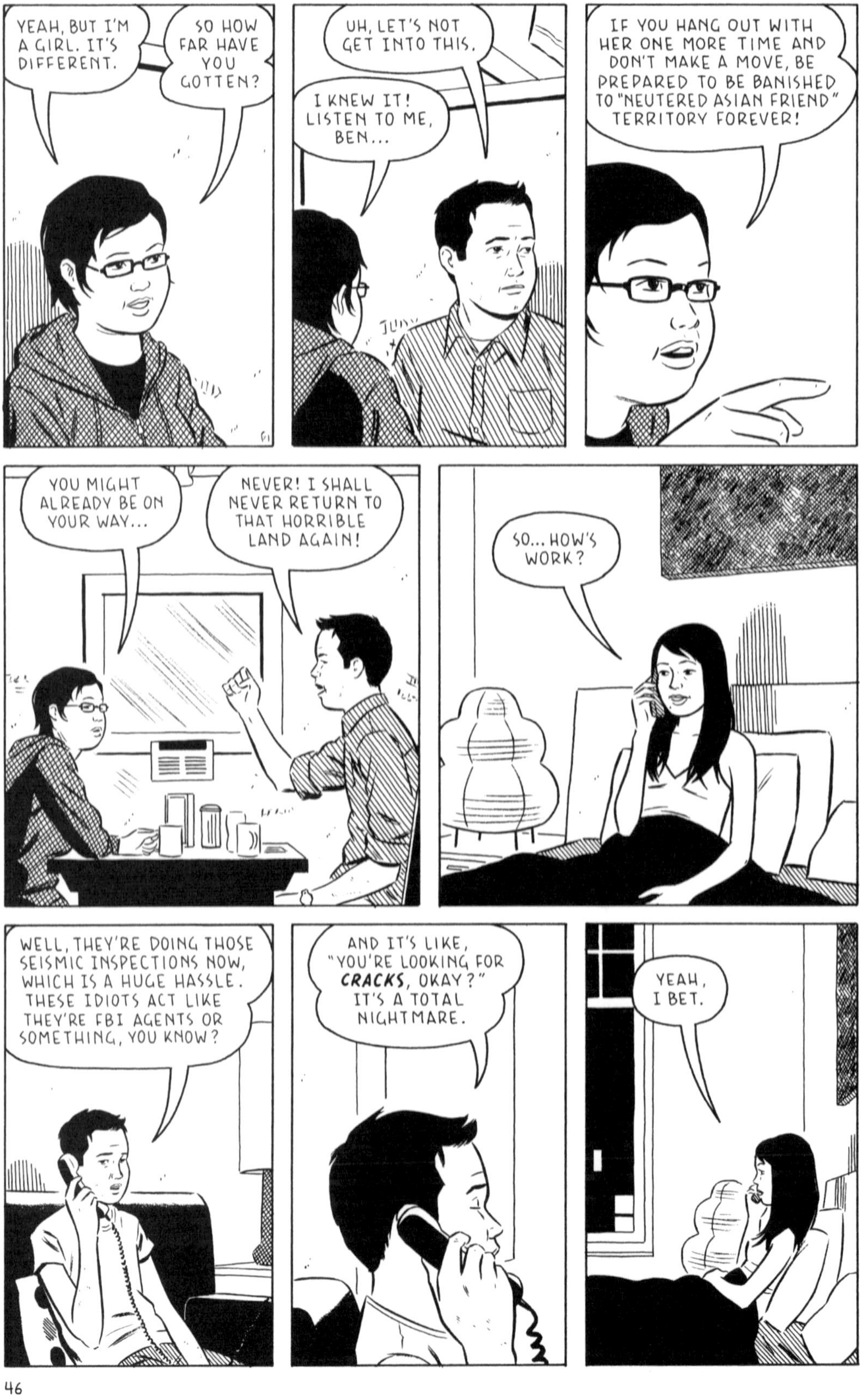
YEAH, BUT I'M A GIRL. IT'S DIFFERENT.
SO HOW FAR HAVE YOU GOTTEN?
UH, LET'S NOT GET INTO THIS.
I KNEW IT! LISTEN TO ME, BEN...
IF YOU HANG OUT WITH HER ONE MORE TIME AND DON'T MAKE A MOVE, BE PREPARED TO BE BANISHED TO "NEUTERED ASIAN FRIEND" TERRITORY FOREVER!
YOU MIGHT ALREADY BE ON YOUR WAY...
NEVER! I SHALL NEVER RETURN TO THAT HORRIBLE LAND AGAIN!
SO... HOW'S WORK?
WELL, THEY'RE DOING THOSE SEISMIC INSPECTIONS NOW, WHICH IS A HUGE HASSLE. THESE IDIOTS ACT LIKE THEY'RE FBI AGENTS OR SOMETHING, YOU KNOW?
AND IT'S LIKE, "YOU'RE LOOKING FOR CRACKS, OKAY?" IT'S A TOTAL NIGHTMARE.
YEAH, I BET.

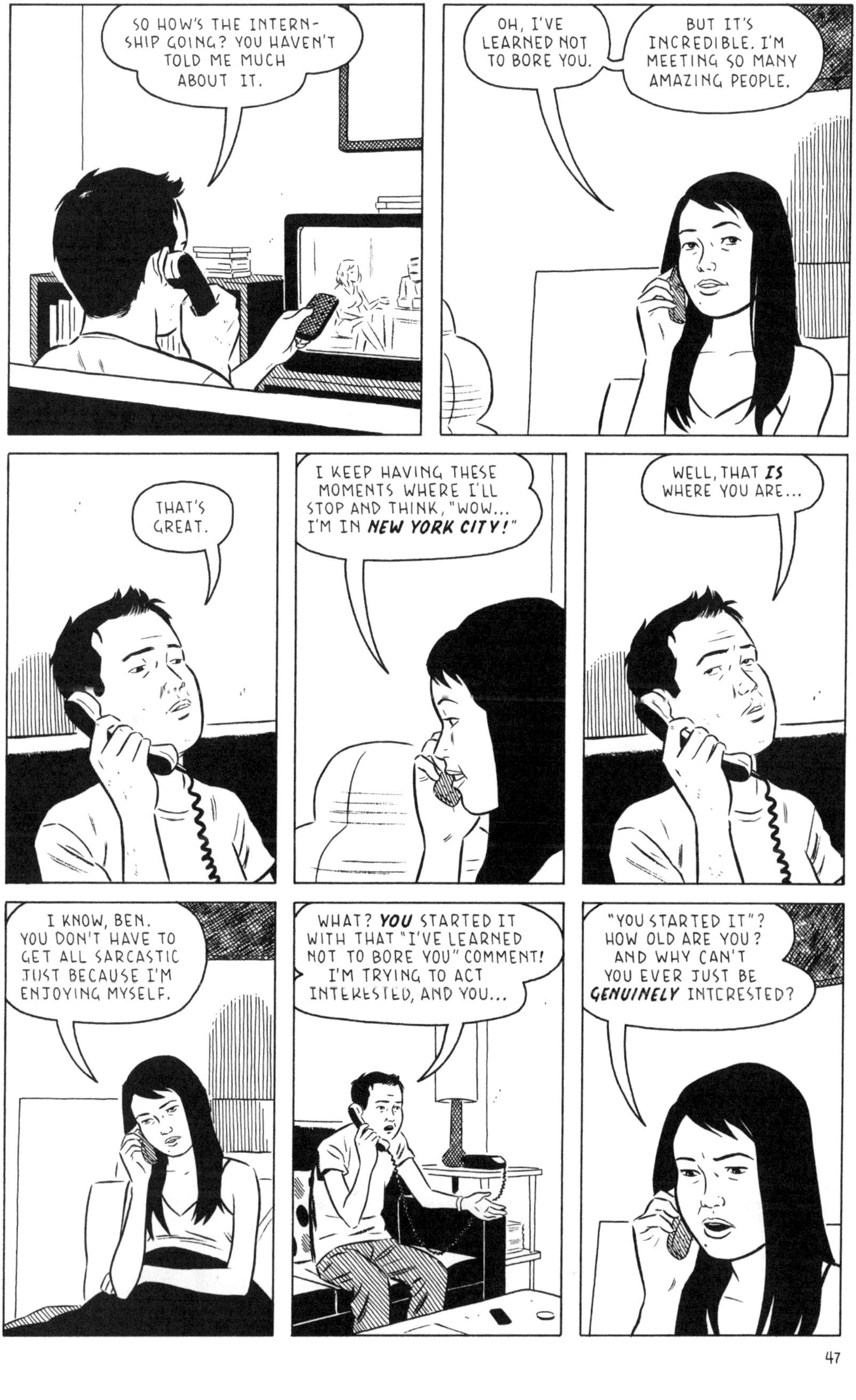
SO HOW'S THE INTERN-SHIP GOING? YOU HAVEN'T TOLD ME MUCH ABOUT IT.
OH, I'VE LEARNED NOT TO BORE YOU.
BUT IT'S INCREDIBLE. I'M MEETING SO MANY AMAZING PEOPLE.
THAT'S GREAT.
I KEEP HAVING THESE MOMENTS WHERE I'LL STOP AND THINK, "WOW... I'M IN **NEW YORK CITY!**"
WELL, THAT **IS** WHERE YOU ARE...
I KNOW, BEN. YOU DON'T HAVE TO GET ALL SARCASTIC JUST BECAUSE I'M ENJOYING MYSELF.
WHAT? **YOU** STARTED IT WITH THAT "I'VE LEARNED NOT TO BORE YOU" COMMENT! I'M TRYING TO ACT INTERESTED, AND YOU...
"YOU STARTED IT"? HOW OLD ARE YOU? AND WHY CAN'T YOU EVER JUST BE **GENUINELY** INTERESTED?

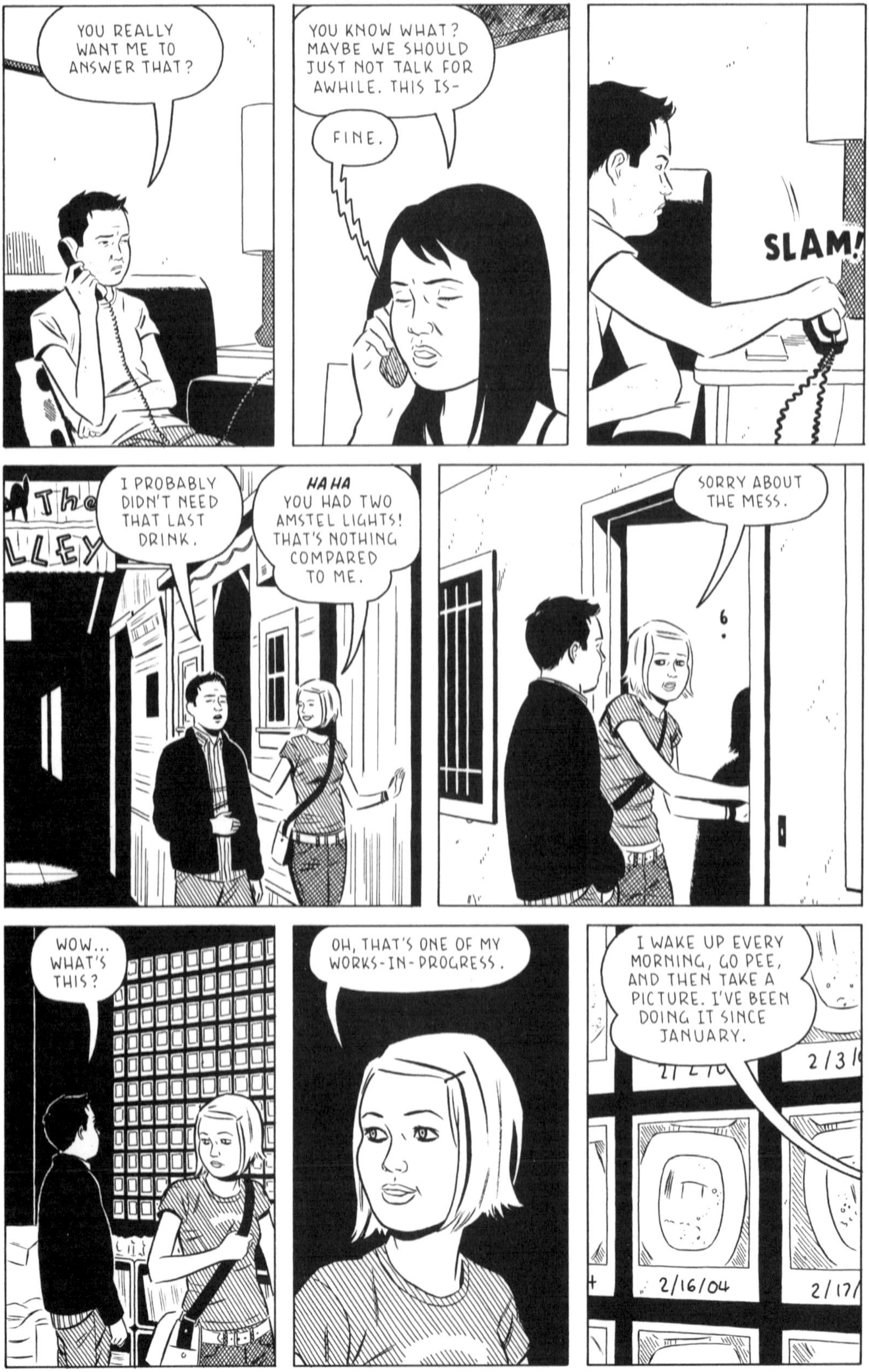
YOU REALLY WANT ME TO ANSWER THAT?
YOU KNOW WHAT? MAYBE WE SHOULD JUST NOT TALK FOR AWHILE. THIS IS-
FINE.
SLAM!
I PROBABLY DIDN'T NEED THAT LAST DRINK.
HA HA YOU HAD TWO AMSTEL LIGHTS! THAT'S NOTHING COMPARED TO ME.
SORRY ABOUT THE MESS.
6
WOW... WHAT'S THIS?
OH, THAT'S ONE OF MY WORKS-IN-PROGRESS.
I WAKE UP EVERY MORNING, GO PEE, AND THEN TAKE A PICTURE. I'VE BEEN DOING IT SINCE JANUARY.
2/16/04

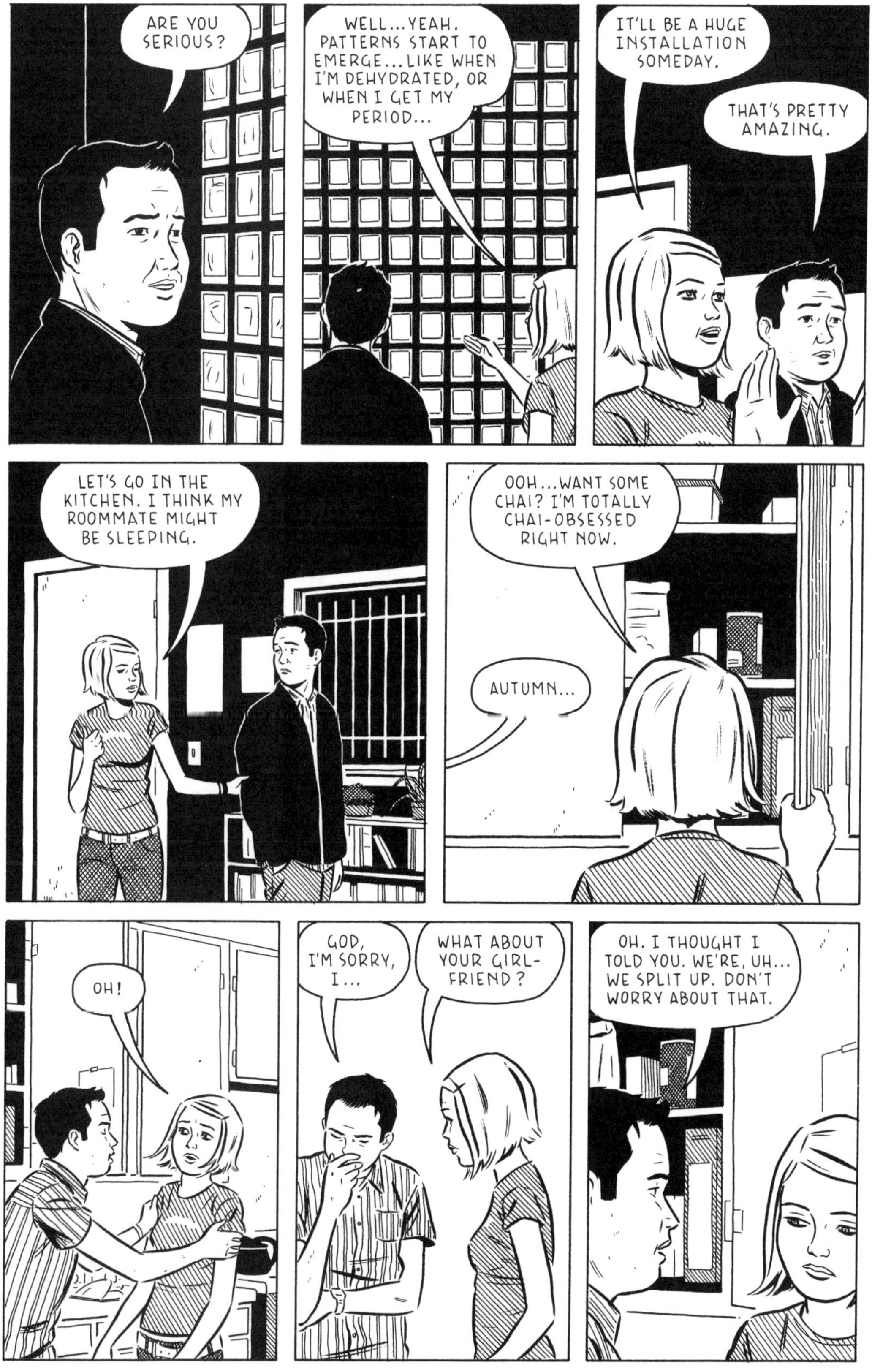
ARE YOU SERIOUS?
WELL...YEAH. PATTERNS START TO EMERGE...LIKE WHEN I'M DEHYDRATED, OR WHEN I GET MY PERIOD...
IT'LL BE A HUGE INSTALLATION SOMEDAY.
THAT'S PRETTY AMAZING.
LET'S GO IN THE KITCHEN. I THINK MY ROOMMATE MIGHT BE SLEEPING.
OOH...WANT SOME CHAI? I'M TOTALLY CHAI-OBSESSED RIGHT NOW.
AUTUMN...
OH!
GOD, I'M SORRY, I...
WHAT ABOUT YOUR GIRL-FRIEND?
OH. I THOUGHT I TOLD YOU. WE'RE, UH... WE SPLIT UP. DON'T WORRY ABOUT THAT.

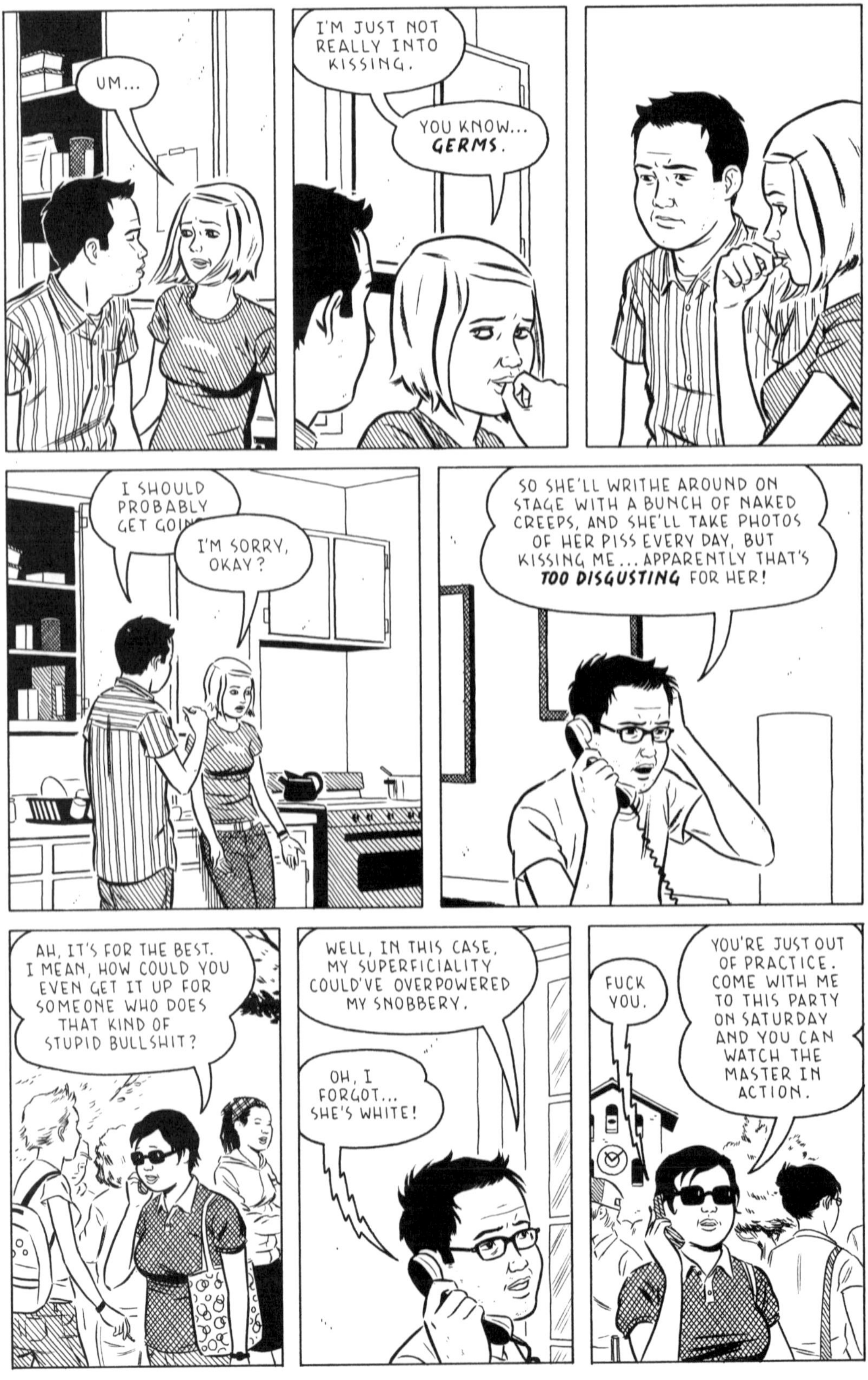
UM...
I'M JUST NOT REALLY INTO KISSING.
YOU KNOW... **GERMS**.
I SHOULD PROBABLY GET GOIN
I'M SORRY, OKAY?
SO SHE'LL WRITHE AROUND ON STAGE WITH A BUNCH OF NAKED CREEPS, AND SHE'LL TAKE PHOTOS OF HER PISS EVERY DAY, BUT KISSING ME... APPARENTLY THAT'S **TOO DISGUSTING** FOR HER!
AH, IT'S FOR THE BEST. I MEAN, HOW COULD YOU EVEN GET IT UP FOR SOMEONE WHO DOES THAT KIND OF STUPID BULLSHIT?
WELL, IN THIS CASE, MY SUPERFICIALITY COULD'VE OVERPOWERED MY SNOBBERY.
OH, I FORGOT... SHE'S WHITE!
FUCK YOU.
YOU'RE JUST OUT OF PRACTICE. COME WITH ME TO THIS PARTY ON SATURDAY AND YOU CAN WATCH THE MASTER IN ACTION.

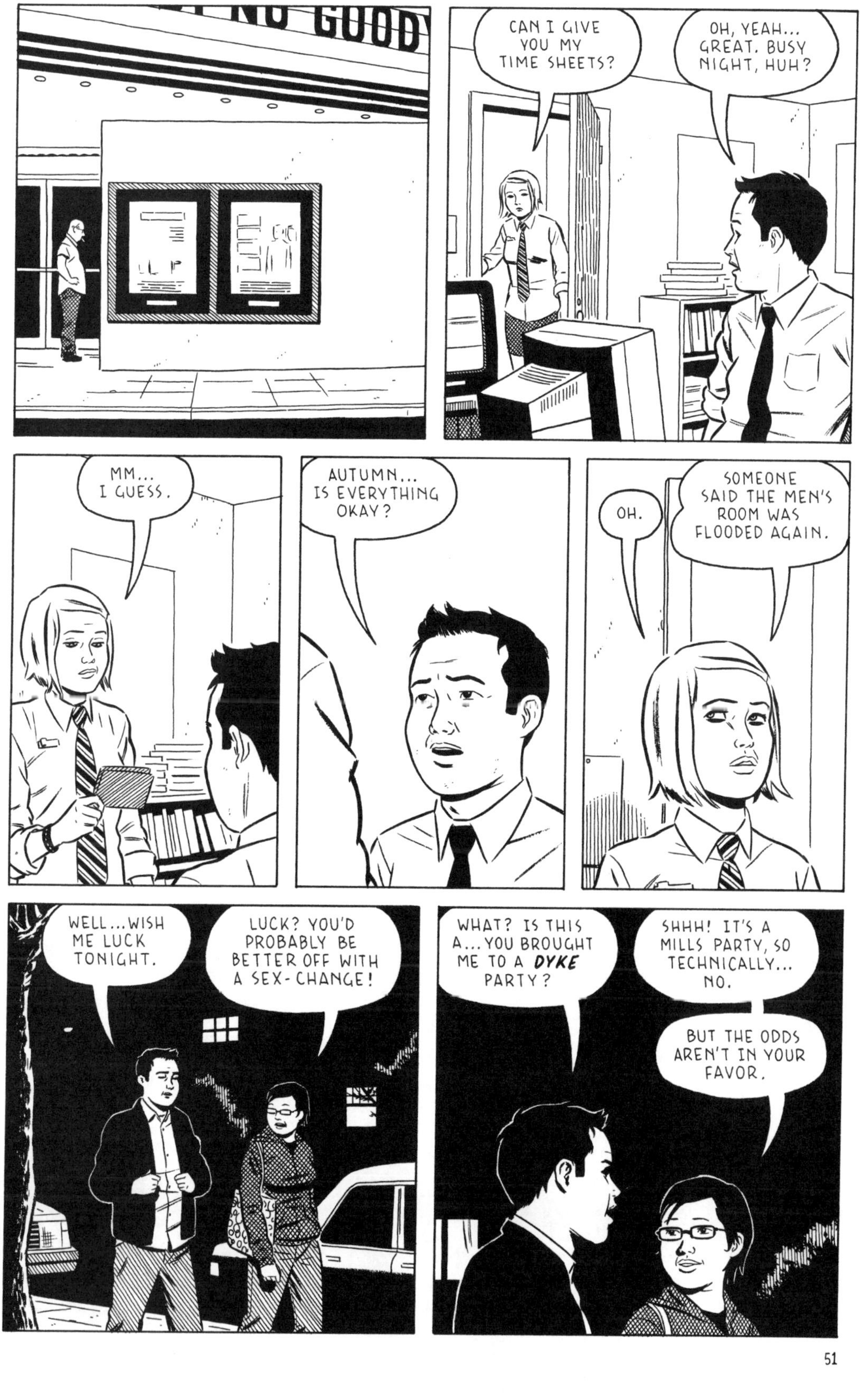
NO GOOD
CAN I GIVE YOU MY TIME SHEETS?
OH, YEAH... GREAT. BUSY NIGHT, HUH?
MM... I GUESS.
AUTUMN... IS EVERYTHING OKAY?
OH.
SOMEONE SAID THE MEN'S ROOM WAS FLOODED AGAIN.
WELL...WISH ME LUCK TONIGHT.
LUCK? YOU'D PROBABLY BE BETTER OFF WITH A SEX-CHANGE!
WHAT? IS THIS A...YOU BROUGHT ME TO A *DYKE* PARTY?
SHHH! IT'S A MILLS PARTY, SO TECHNICALLY... NO.
BUT THE ODDS AREN'T IN YOUR FAVOR.

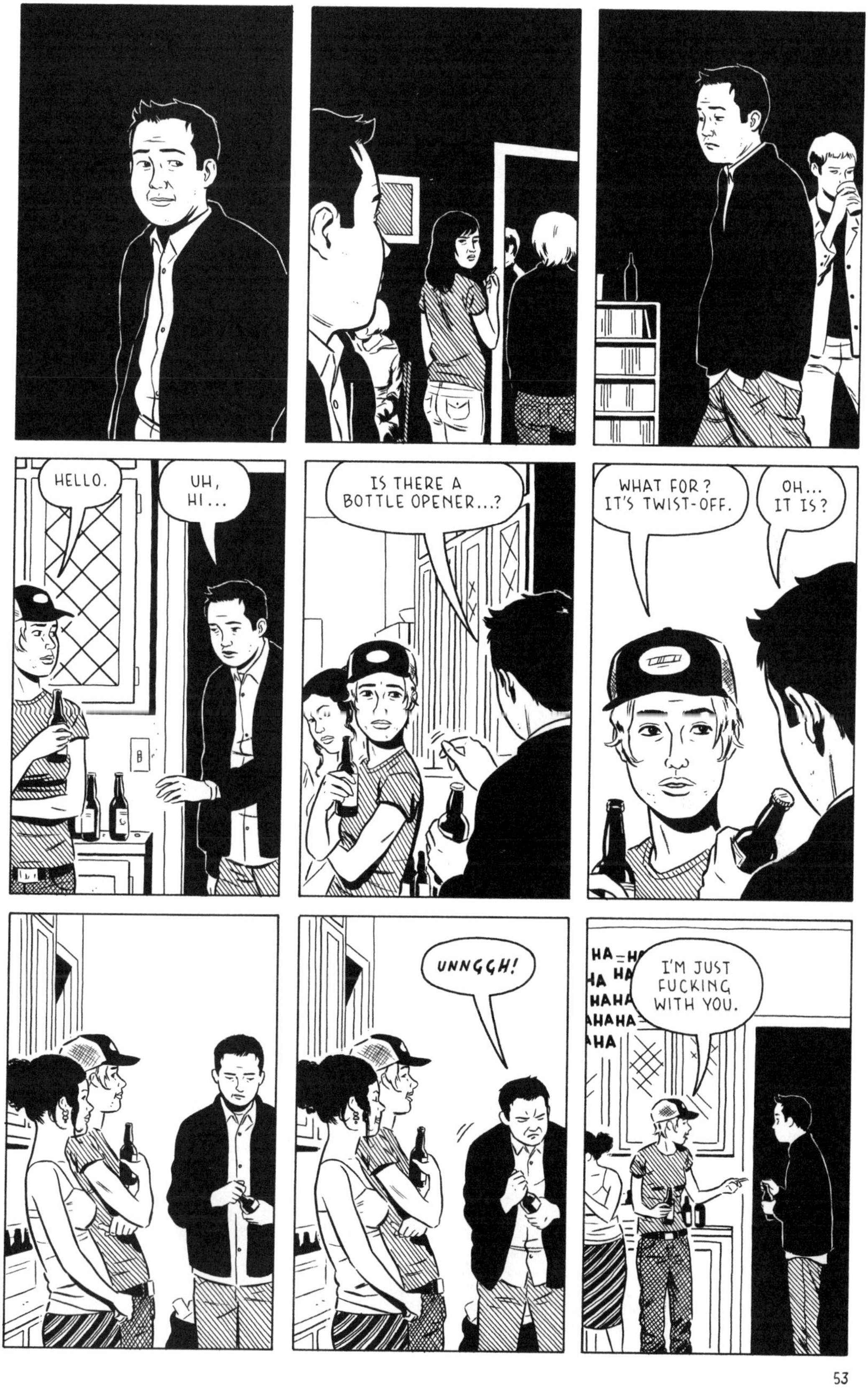
HELLO.
UH, HI...
IS THERE A BOTTLE OPENER...?
WHAT FOR? IT'S TWIST-OFF.
OH... IT IS?
UNNGGH!
HA HA HA HA HAHA AHAHA HA
I'M JUST FUCKING WITH YOU.

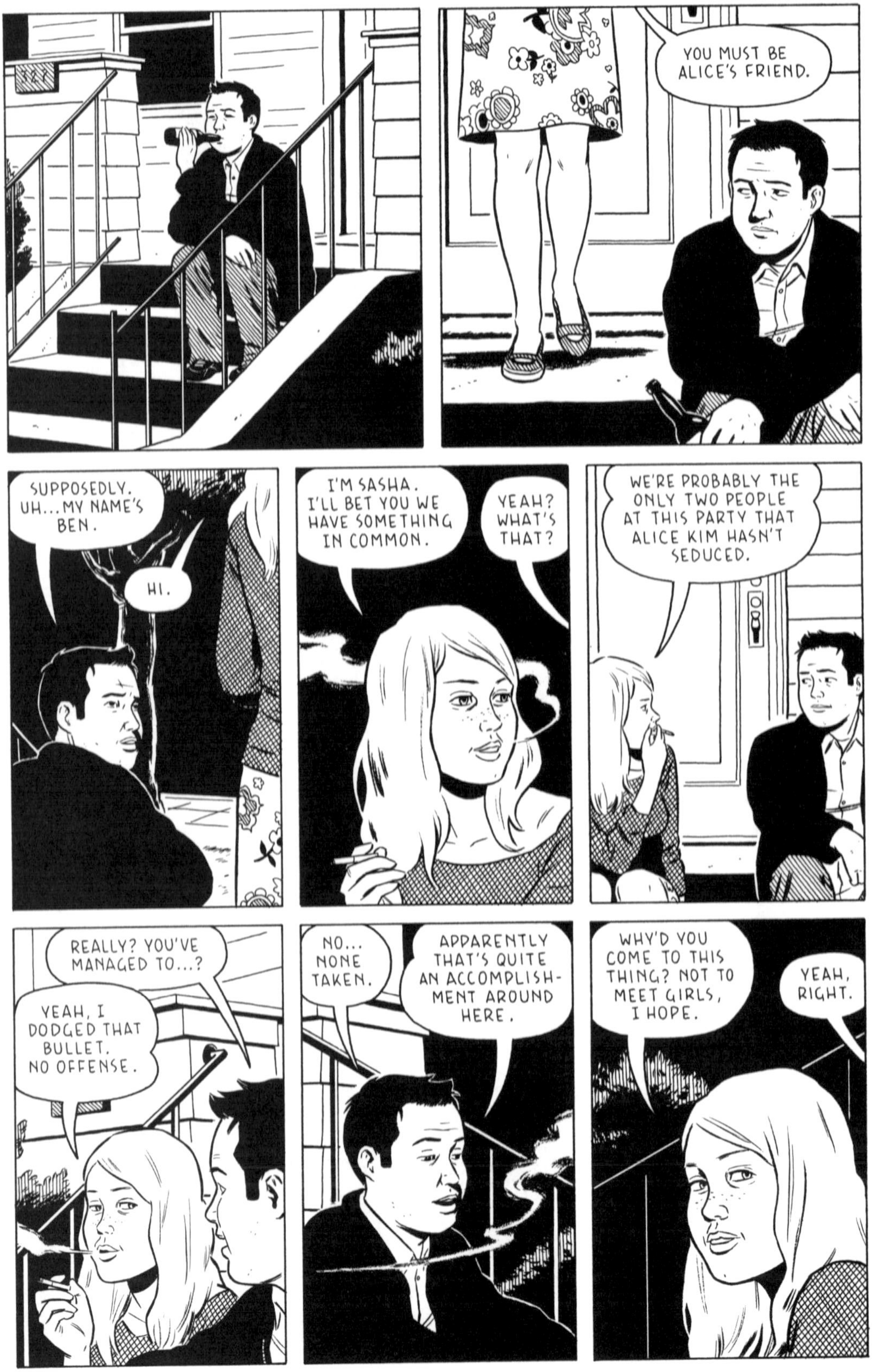
YOU MUST BE ALICE'S FRIEND.
SUPPOSEDLY. UH... MY NAME'S BEN.
HI.
I'M SASHA. I'LL BET YOU WE HAVE SOMETHING IN COMMON.
YEAH? WHAT'S THAT?
WE'RE PROBABLY THE ONLY TWO PEOPLE AT THIS PARTY THAT ALICE KIM HASN'T SEDUCED.
REALLY? YOU'VE MANAGED TO...?
YEAH, I DODGED THAT BULLET. NO OFFENSE.
NO... NONE TAKEN.
APPARENTLY THAT'S QUITE AN ACCOMPLISH-MENT AROUND HERE.
WHY'D YOU COME TO THIS THING? NOT TO MEET GIRLS, I HOPE.
YEAH, RIGHT.

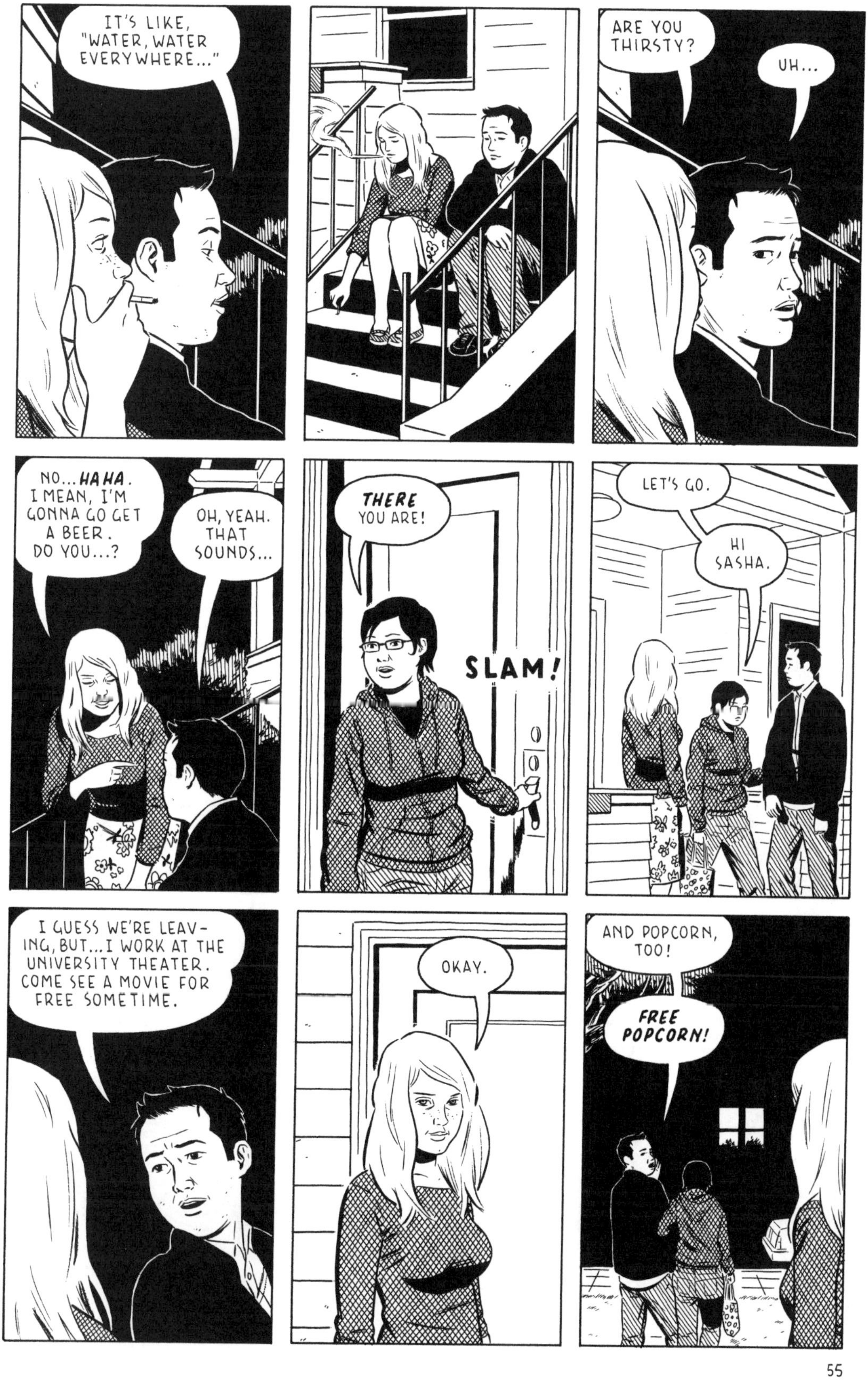
IT'S LIKE, "WATER, WATER EVERYWHERE..."
ARE YOU THIRSTY?
UH...
NO... HAHA. I MEAN, I'M GONNA GO GET A BEER. DO YOU...?
OH, YEAH. THAT SOUNDS...
THERE YOU ARE!
SLAM!
LET'S GO.
HI SASHA.
I GUESS WE'RE LEAVING, BUT... I WORK AT THE UNIVERSITY THEATER. COME SEE A MOVIE FOR FREE SOMETIME.
OKAY.
AND POPCORN, TOO!
FREE POPCORN!

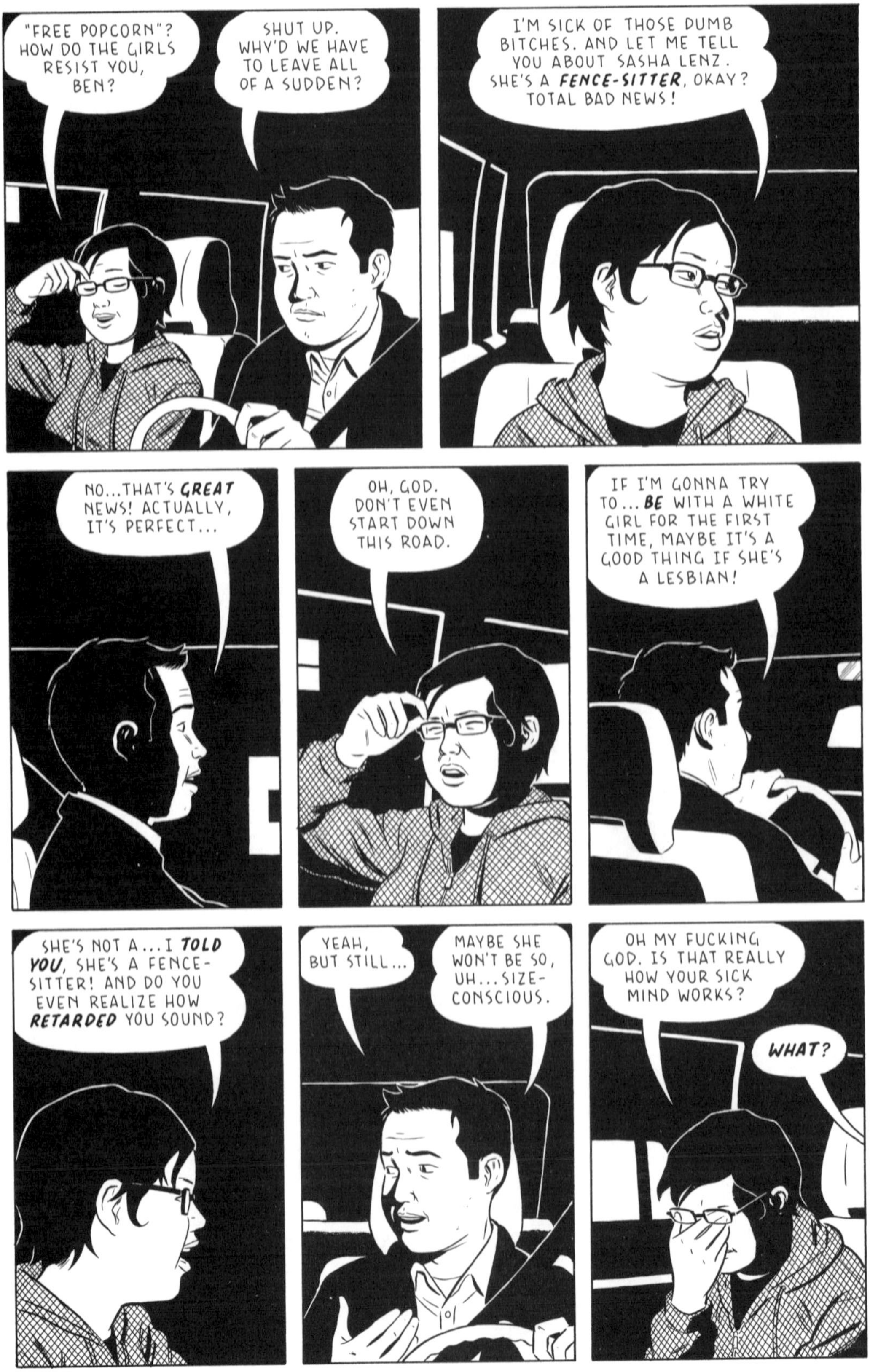
"FREE POPCORN"? HOW DO THE GIRLS RESIST YOU, BEN?
SHUT UP. WHY'D WE HAVE TO LEAVE ALL OF A SUDDEN?
I'M SICK OF THOSE DUMB BITCHES. AND LET ME TELL YOU ABOUT SASHA LENZ. SHE'S A **FENCE-SITTER**, OKAY? TOTAL BAD NEWS!
NO...THAT'S **GREAT** NEWS! ACTUALLY, IT'S PERFECT...
OH, GOD. DON'T EVEN START DOWN THIS ROAD.
IF I'M GONNA TRY TO... **BE** WITH A WHITE GIRL FOR THE FIRST TIME, MAYBE IT'S A GOOD THING IF SHE'S A LESBIAN!
SHE'S NOT A... I **TOLD YOU**, SHE'S A FENCE-SITTER! AND DO YOU EVEN REALIZE HOW **RETARDED** YOU SOUND?
YEAH, BUT STILL...
MAYBE SHE WON'T BE SO, UH... SIZE-CONSCIOUS.
OH MY FUCKING GOD. IS THAT REALLY HOW YOUR SICK MIND WORKS?
WHAT?

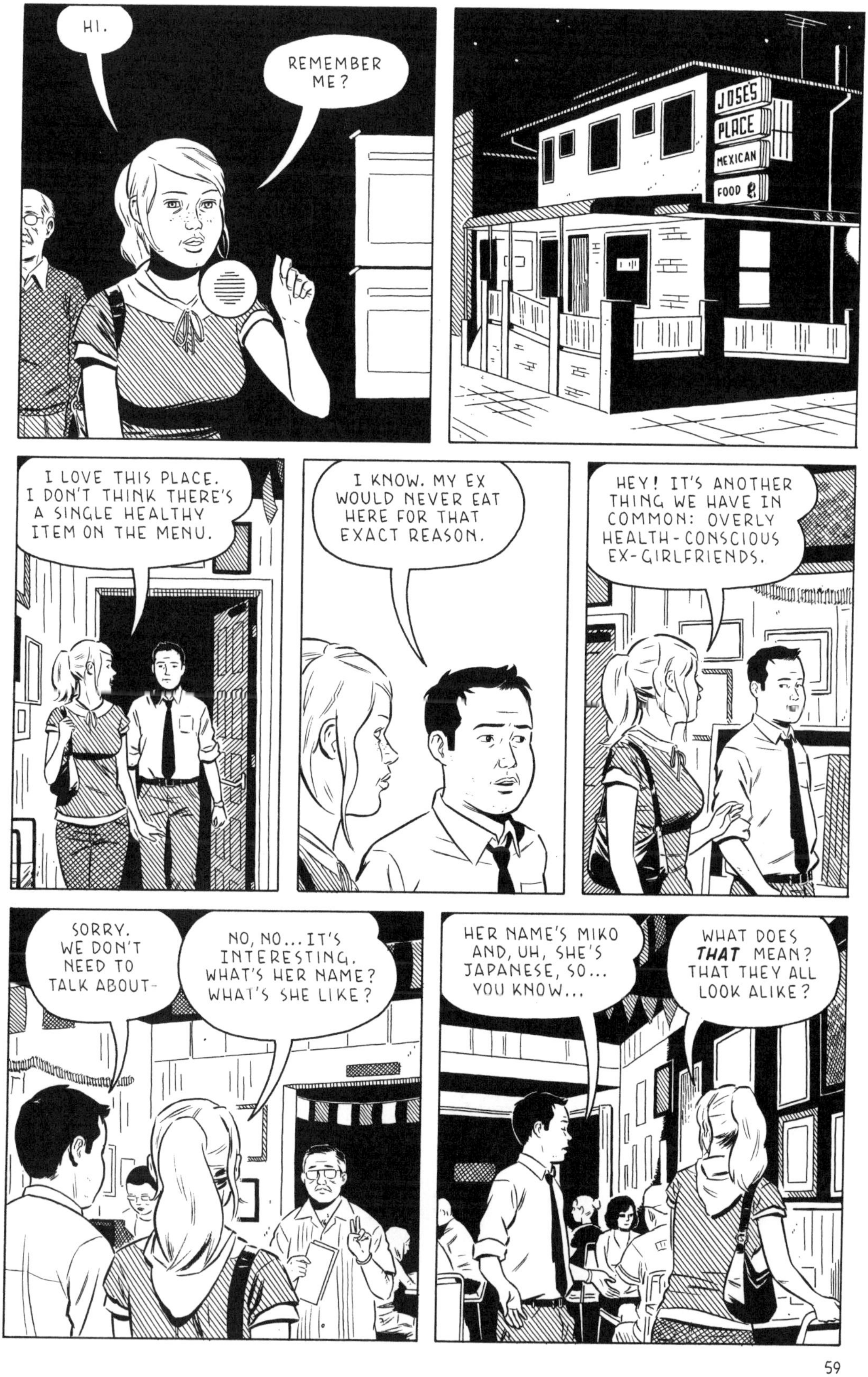
HI.
REMEMBER ME?
JOSE'S PLACE
MEXICAN FOOD
I LOVE THIS PLACE. I DON'T THINK THERE'S A SINGLE HEALTHY ITEM ON THE MENU.
I KNOW. MY EX WOULD NEVER EAT HERE FOR THAT EXACT REASON.
HEY! IT'S ANOTHER THING WE HAVE IN COMMON: OVERLY HEALTH-CONSCIOUS EX-GIRLFRIENDS.
SORRY. WE DON'T NEED TO TALK ABOUT-
NO, NO... IT'S INTERESTING. WHAT'S HER NAME? WHAT'S SHE LIKE?
HER NAME'S MIKO AND, UH, SHE'S JAPANESE, SO... YOU KNOW...
WHAT DOES **THAT** MEAN? THAT THEY ALL LOOK ALIKE?

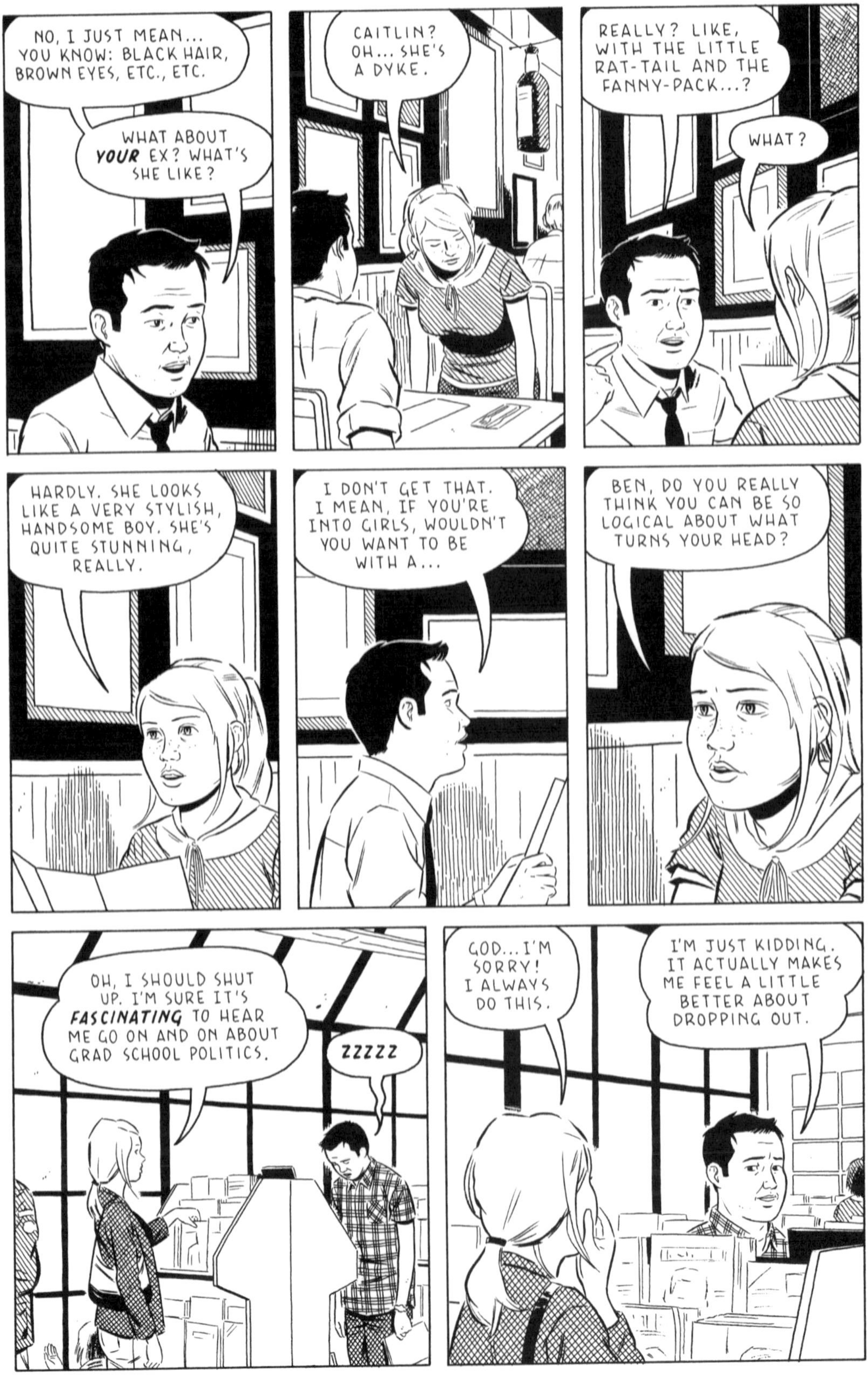

NO, I JUST MEAN... YOU KNOW: BLACK HAIR, BROWN EYES, ETC., ETC.
WHAT ABOUT **YOUR** EX? WHAT'S SHE LIKE?
CAITLIN? OH... SHE'S A DYKE.
REALLY? LIKE, WITH THE LITTLE RAT-TAIL AND THE FANNY-PACK...?
WHAT?
HARDLY. SHE LOOKS LIKE A VERY STYLISH, HANDSOME BOY. SHE'S QUITE STUNNING, REALLY.
I DON'T GET THAT. I MEAN, IF YOU'RE INTO GIRLS, WOULDN'T YOU WANT TO BE WITH A...
BEN, DO YOU REALLY THINK YOU CAN BE SO LOGICAL ABOUT WHAT TURNS YOUR HEAD?
OH, I SHOULD SHUT UP. I'M SURE IT'S **FASCINATING** TO HEAR ME GO ON AND ON ABOUT GRAD SCHOOL POLITICS.
ZZZZZ
GOD... I'M SORRY! I ALWAYS DO THIS.
I'M JUST KIDDING. IT ACTUALLY MAKES ME FEEL A LITTLE BETTER ABOUT DROPPING OUT.

61

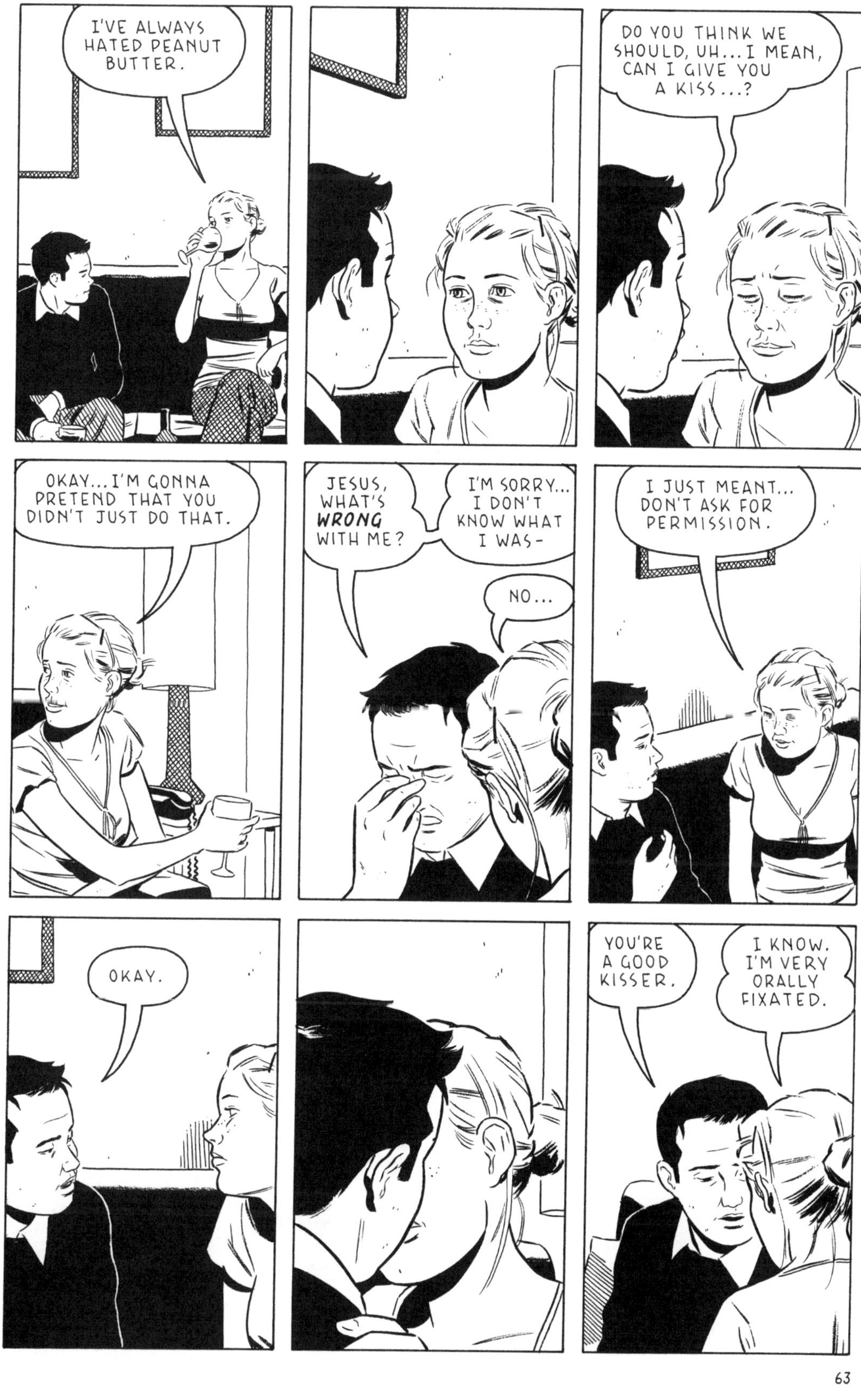
I'VE ALWAYS HATED PEANUT BUTTER.
DO YOU THINK WE SHOULD, UH... I MEAN, CAN I GIVE YOU A KISS...?
OKAY... I'M GONNA PRETEND THAT YOU DIDN'T JUST DO THAT.
JESUS, WHAT'S **WRONG** WITH ME?
I'M SORRY... I DON'T KNOW WHAT I WAS-
NO...
I JUST MEANT... DON'T ASK FOR PERMISSION.
OKAY.
YOU'RE A GOOD KISSER.
I KNOW. I'M VERY ORALLY FIXATED.

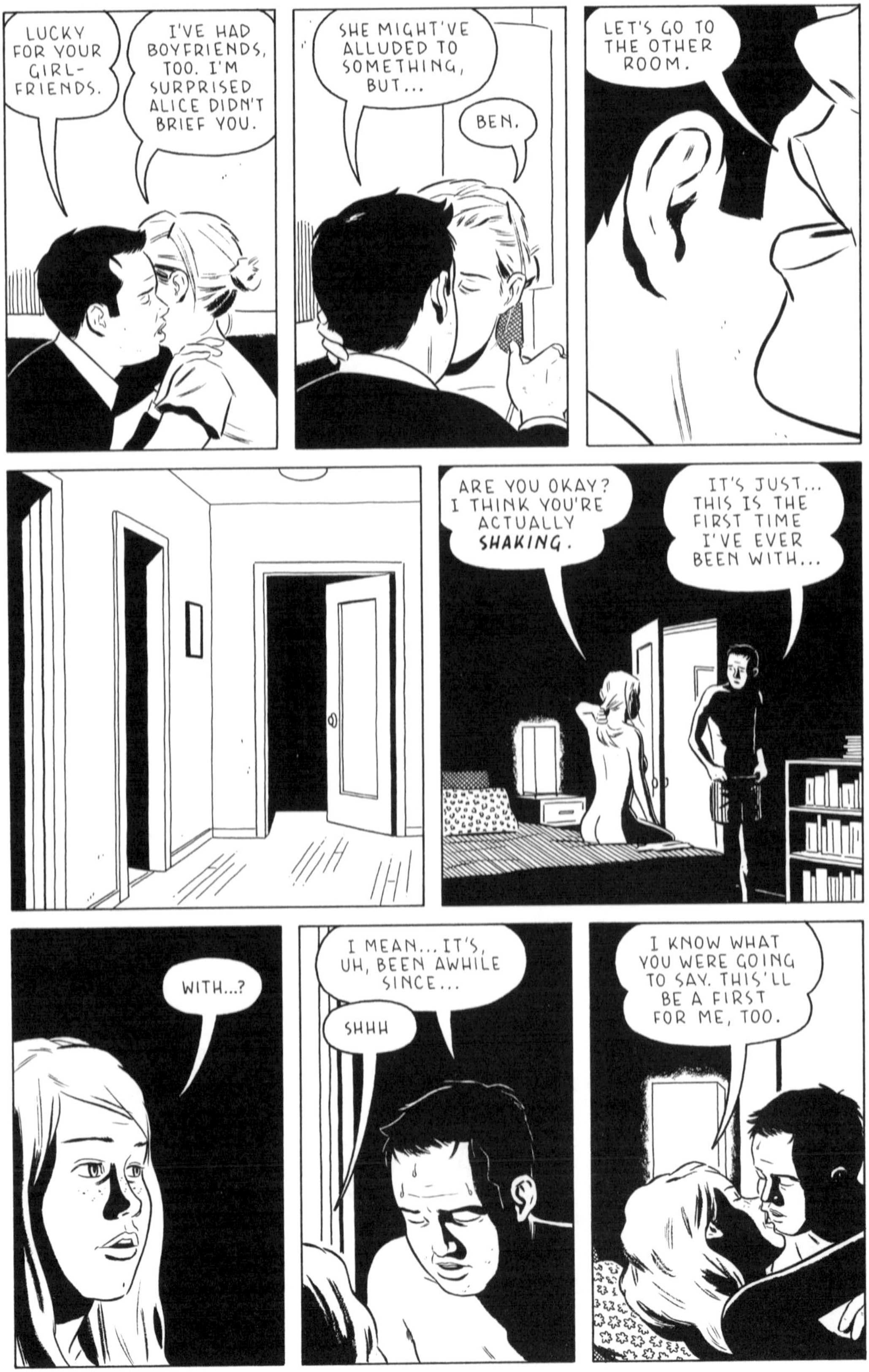
LUCKY FOR YOUR GIRL-FRIENDS.
I'VE HAD BOYFRIENDS, TOO. I'M SURPRISED ALICE DIDN'T BRIEF YOU.
SHE MIGHT'VE ALLUDED TO SOMETHING, BUT...
BEN.
LET'S GO TO THE OTHER ROOM.
ARE YOU OKAY? I THINK YOU'RE ACTUALLY **SHAKING**.
IT'S JUST... THIS IS THE FIRST TIME I'VE EVER BEEN WITH...
WITH...?
I MEAN... IT'S, UH, BEEN AWHILE SINCE...
SHHH
I KNOW WHAT YOU WERE GOING TO SAY. THIS'LL BE A FIRST FOR ME, TOO.

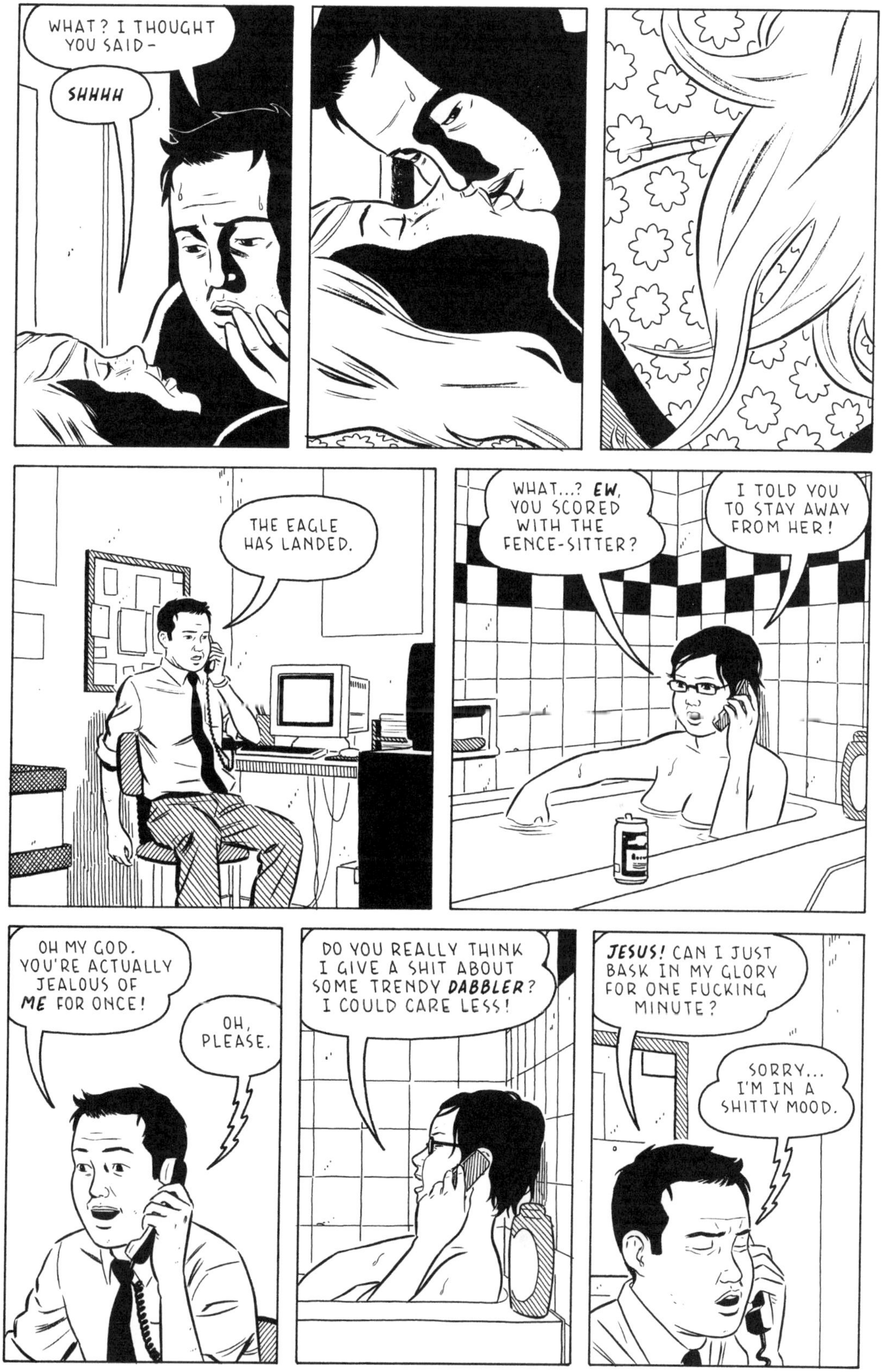
WHAT? I THOUGHT YOU SAID-
SHHHH
THE EAGLE HAS LANDED.
WHAT...? EW, YOU SCORED WITH THE FENCE-SITTER?
I TOLD YOU TO STAY AWAY FROM HER!
OH MY GOD. YOU'RE ACTUALLY JEALOUS OF ME FOR ONCE!
OH, PLEASE.
DO YOU REALLY THINK I GIVE A SHIT ABOUT SOME TRENDY DABBLER? I COULD CARE LESS!
JESUS! CAN I JUST BASK IN MY GLORY FOR ONE FUCKING MINUTE?
SORRY... I'M IN A SHITTY MOOD.

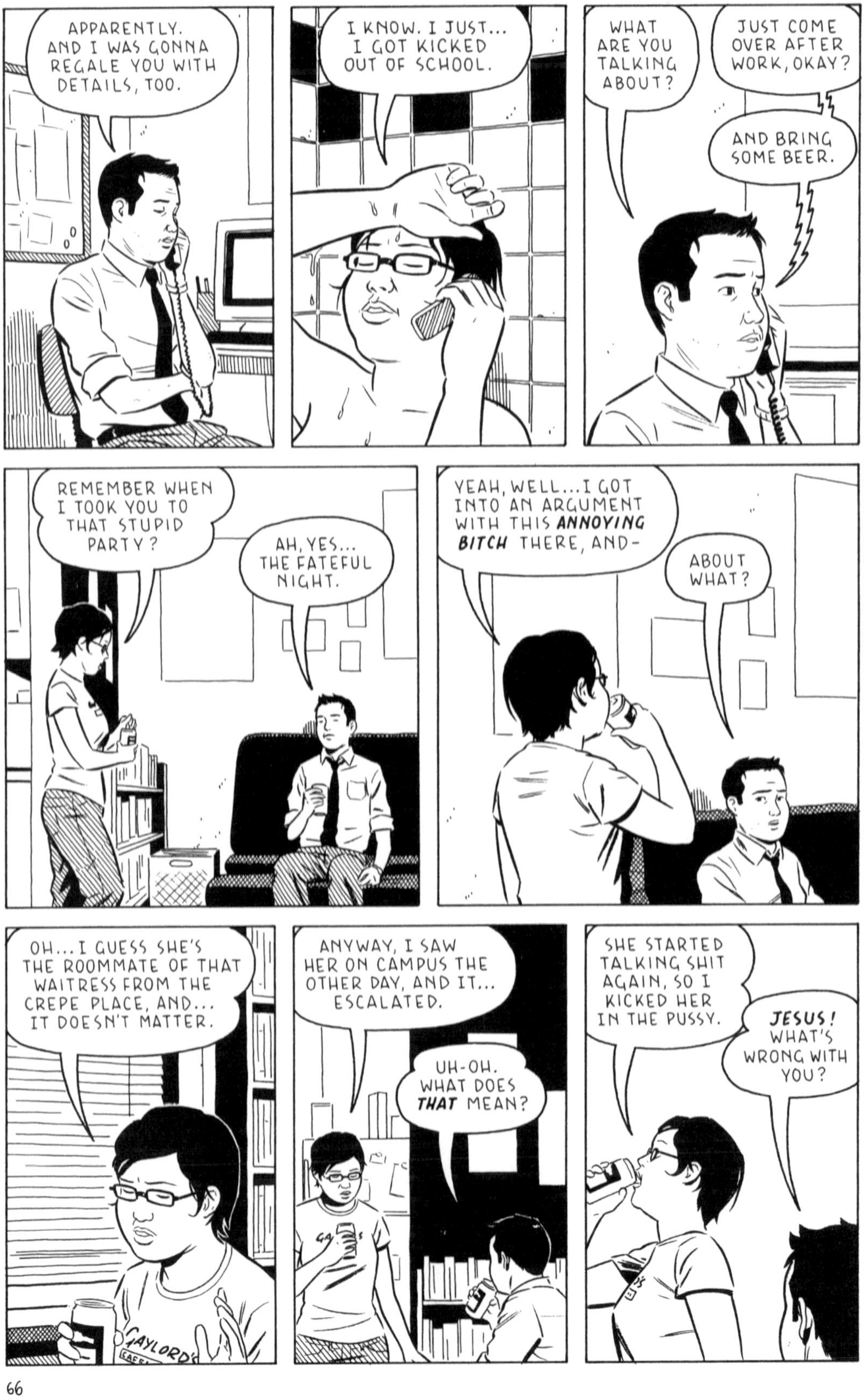
APPARENTLY. AND I WAS GONNA REGALE YOU WITH DETAILS, TOO.
I KNOW. I JUST... I GOT KICKED OUT OF SCHOOL.
WHAT ARE YOU TALKING ABOUT?
JUST COME OVER AFTER WORK, OKAY?
AND BRING SOME BEER.
REMEMBER WHEN I TOOK YOU TO THAT STUPID PARTY?
AH, YES... THE FATEFUL NIGHT.
YEAH, WELL... I GOT INTO AN ARGUMENT WITH THIS **ANNOYING BITCH** THERE, AND-
ABOUT WHAT?
OH... I GUESS SHE'S THE ROOMMATE OF THAT WAITRESS FROM THE CREPE PLACE, AND... IT DOESN'T MATTER.
GAYLORD'S
ANYWAY, I SAW HER ON CAMPUS THE OTHER DAY, AND IT... ESCALATED.
UH-OH. WHAT DOES **THAT** MEAN?
SHE STARTED TALKING SHIT AGAIN, SO I KICKED HER IN THE PUSSY.
JESUS! WHAT'S WRONG WITH YOU?

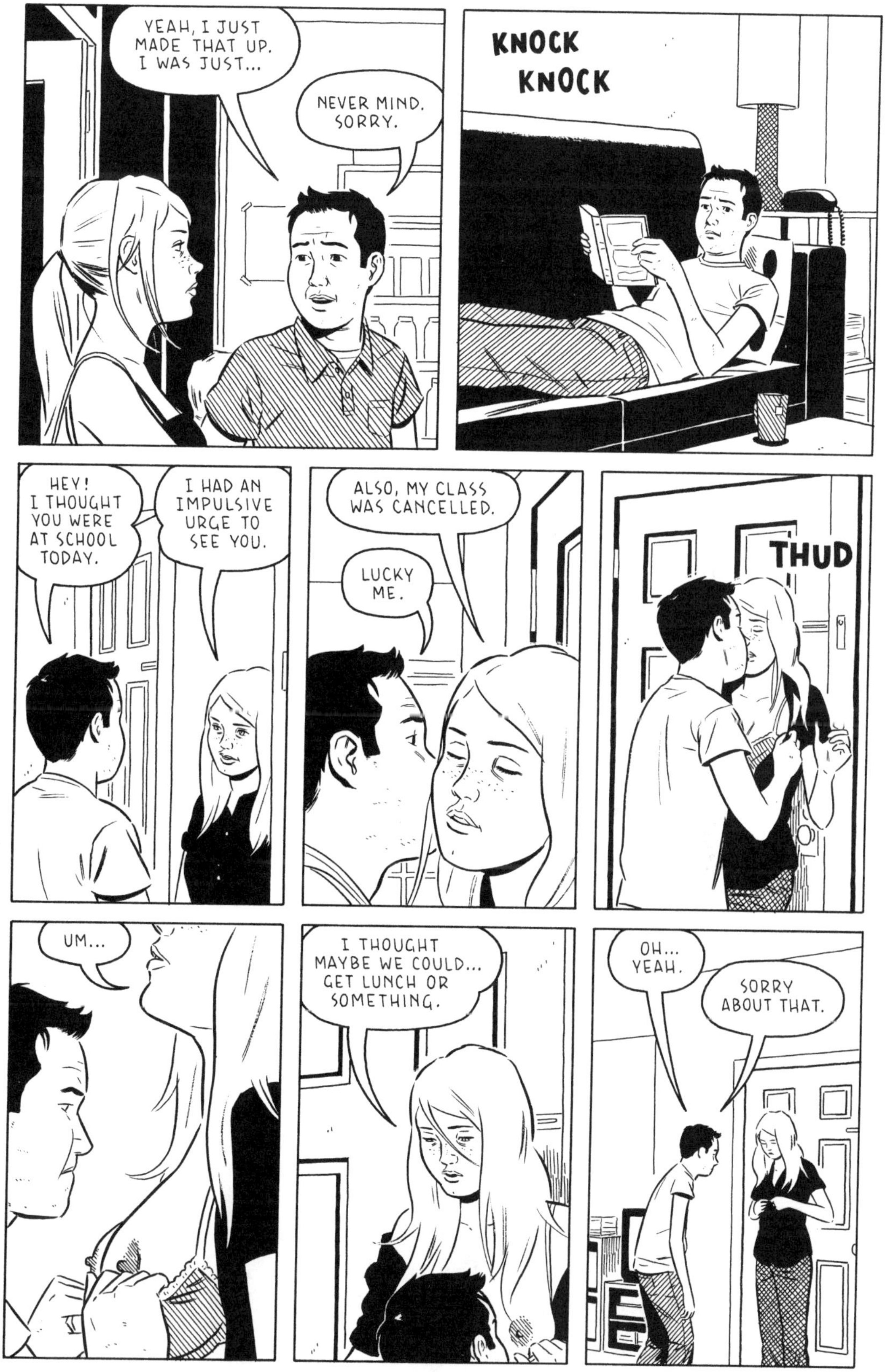
YEAH, I JUST MADE THAT UP. I WAS JUST...
NEVER MIND. SORRY.
KNOCK KNOCK
HEY! I THOUGHT YOU WERE AT SCHOOL TODAY.
I HAD AN IMPULSIVE URGE TO SEE YOU.
ALSO, MY CLASS WAS CANCELLED.
LUCKY ME.
THUD
UM...
I THOUGHT MAYBE WE COULD... GET LUNCH OR SOMETHING.
OH... YEAH.
SORRY ABOUT THAT.

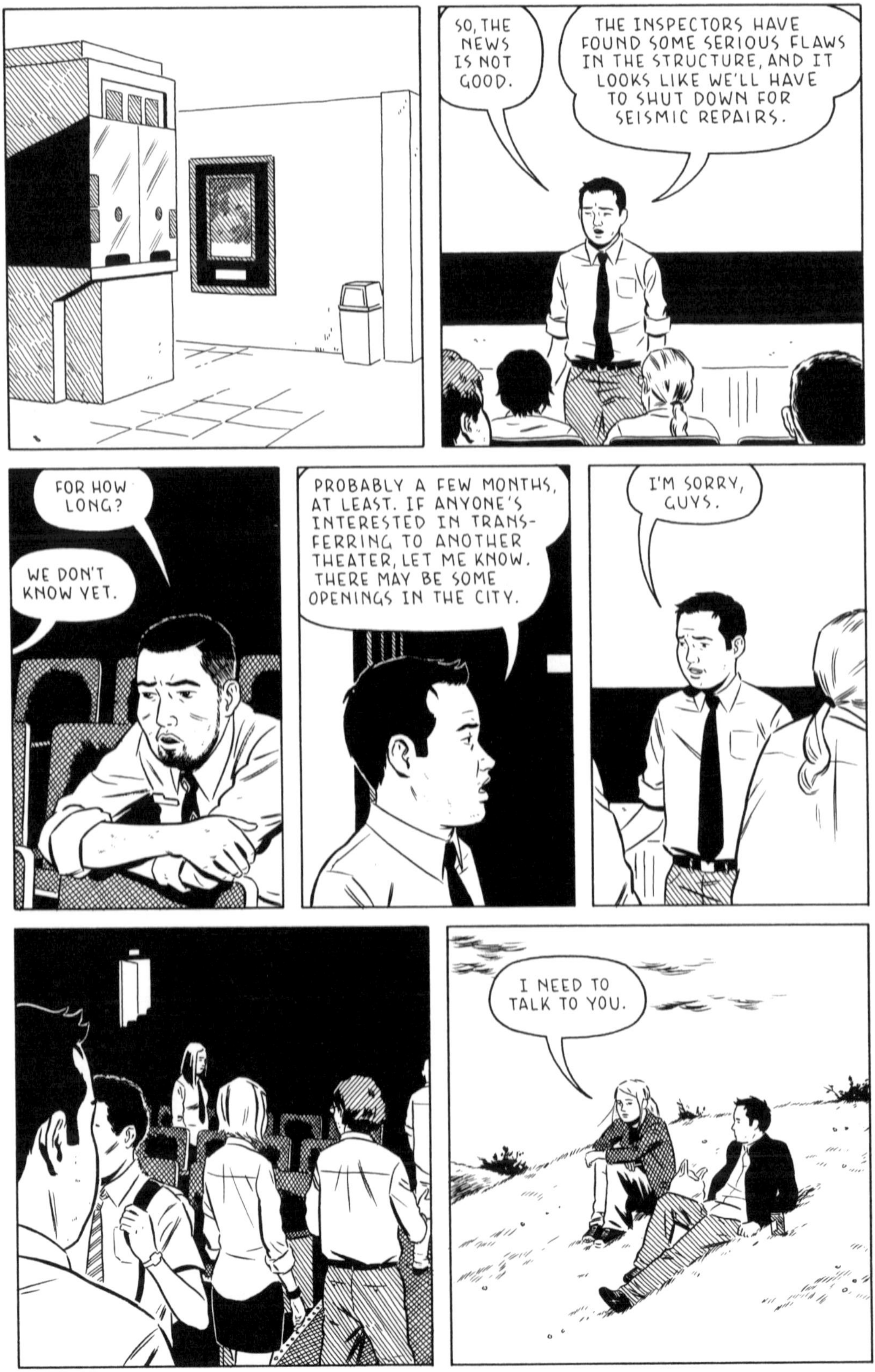
SO, THE NEWS IS NOT GOOD.
THE INSPECTORS HAVE FOUND SOME SERIOUS FLAWS IN THE STRUCTURE, AND IT LOOKS LIKE WE'LL HAVE TO SHUT DOWN FOR SEISMIC REPAIRS.
FOR HOW LONG?
WE DON'T KNOW YET.
PROBABLY A FEW MONTHS, AT LEAST. IF ANYONE'S INTERESTED IN TRANS-FERRING TO ANOTHER THEATER, LET ME KNOW. THERE MAY BE SOME OPENINGS IN THE CITY.
I'M SORRY, GUYS.
I NEED TO TALK TO YOU.

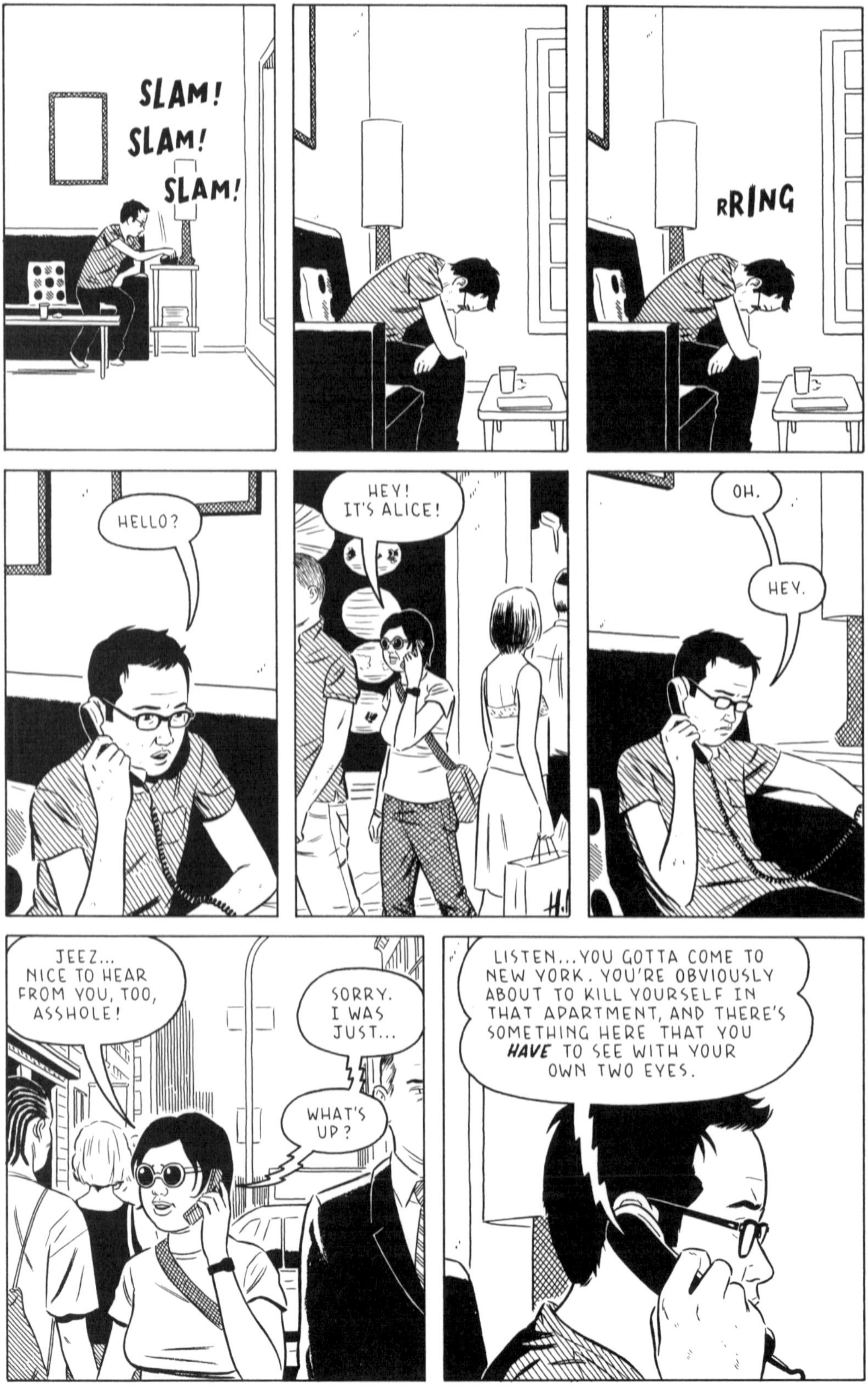
SLAM!
SLAM!
SLAM!
RRING
HELLO?
HEY! IT'S ALICE!
OH.
HEY.
JEEZ... NICE TO HEAR FROM YOU, TOO, ASSHOLE!
SORRY. I WAS JUST...
WHAT'S UP?
LISTEN... YOU GOTTA COME TO NEW YORK. YOU'RE OBVIOUSLY ABOUT TO KILL YOURSELF IN THAT APARTMENT, AND THERE'S SOMETHING HERE THAT YOU ***HAVE*** TO SEE WITH YOUR OWN TWO EYES.

CHAPTER THREE

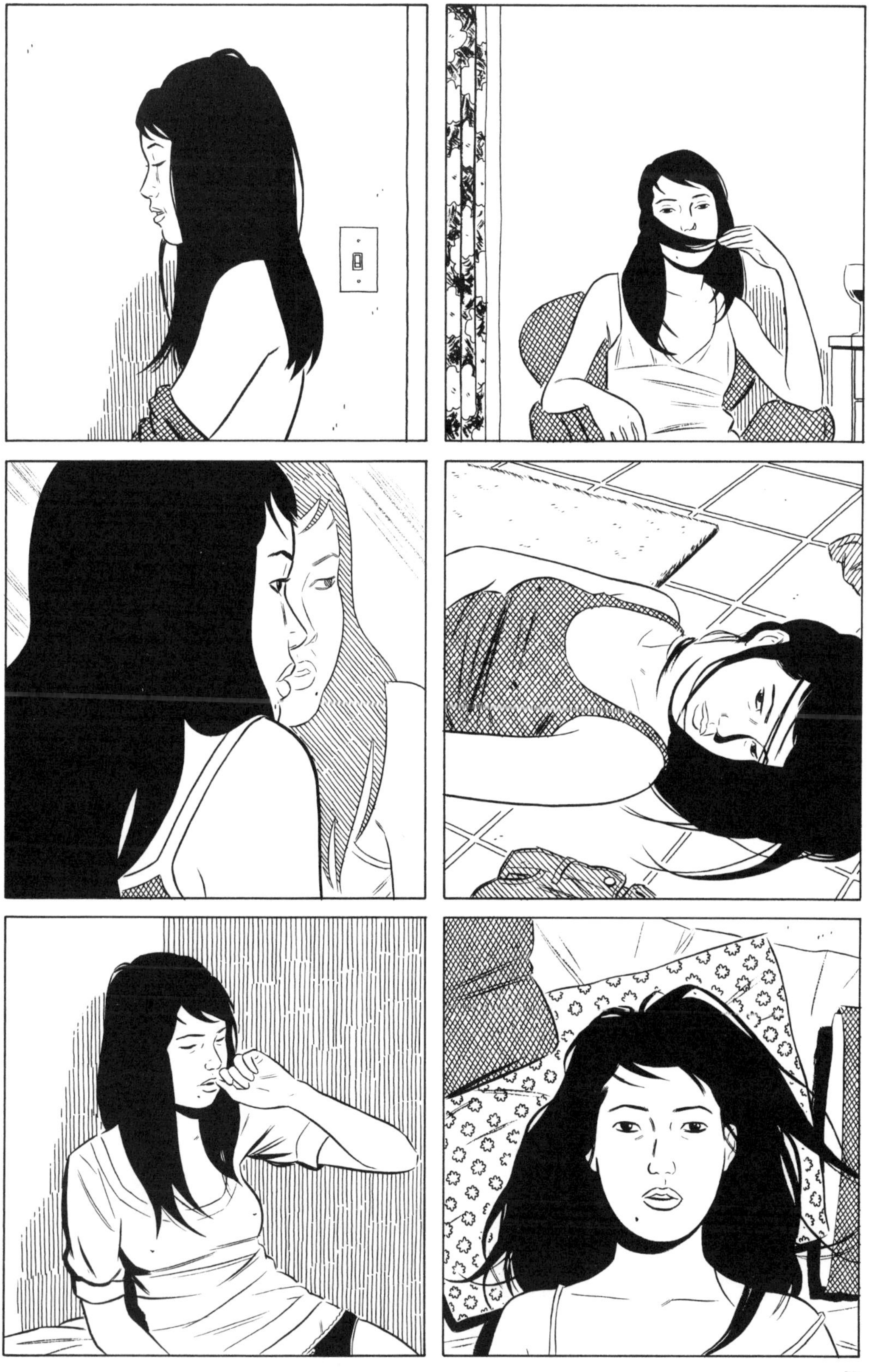

82

83

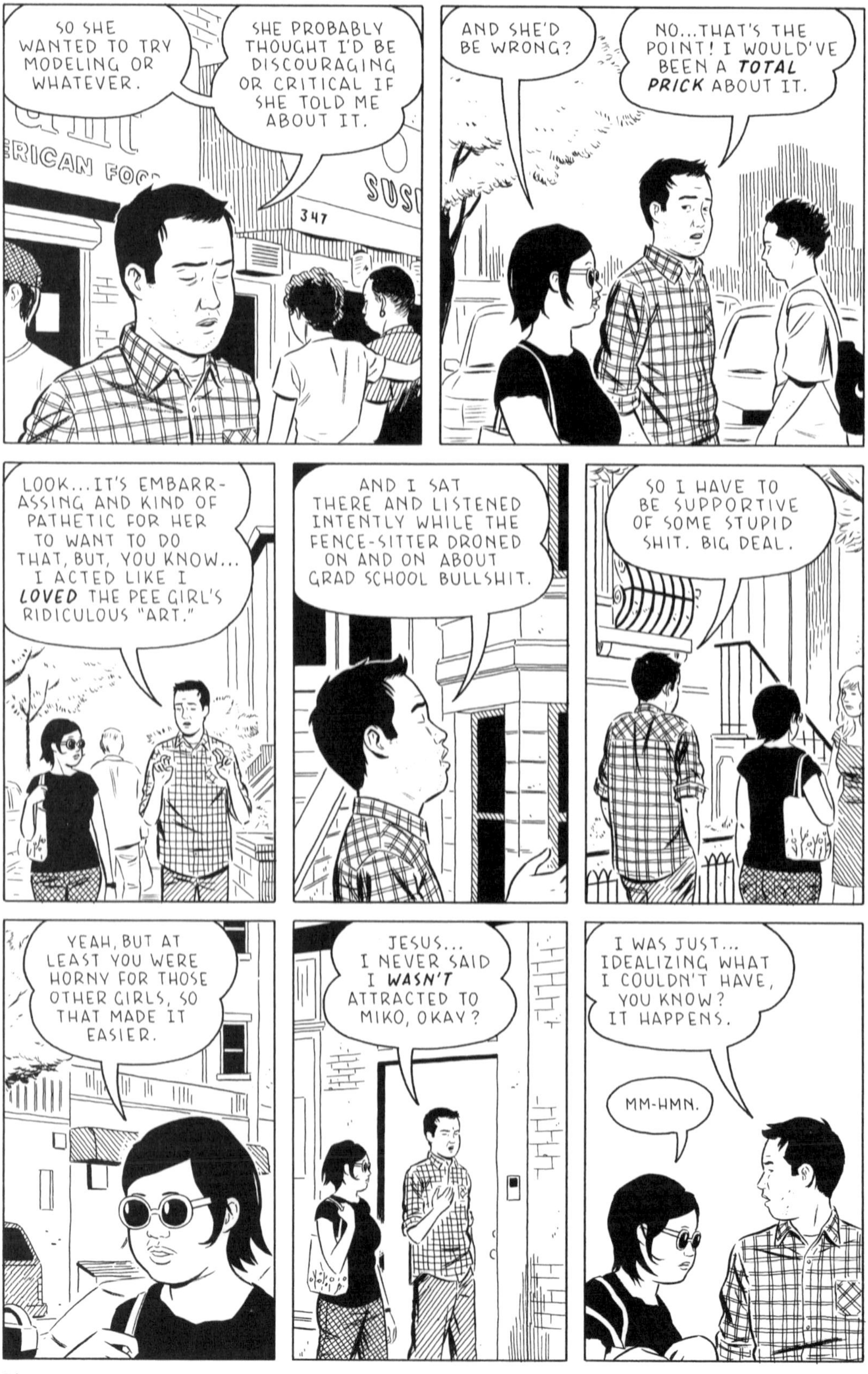
SO SHE WANTED TO TRY MODELING OR WHATEVER.
SHE PROBABLY THOUGHT I'D BE DISCOURAGING OR CRITICAL IF SHE TOLD ME ABOUT IT.
ERICAN FOO
SUS
347
AND SHE'D BE WRONG?
NO... THAT'S THE POINT! I WOULD'VE BEEN A TOTAL PRICK ABOUT IT.
LOOK... IT'S EMBARRASSING AND KIND OF PATHETIC FOR HER TO WANT TO DO THAT, BUT, YOU KNOW... I ACTED LIKE I LOVED THE PEE GIRL'S RIDICULOUS "ART."
AND I SAT THERE AND LISTENED INTENTLY WHILE THE FENCE-SITTER DRONED ON AND ON ABOUT GRAD SCHOOL BULLSHIT.
SO I HAVE TO BE SUPPORTIVE OF SOME STUPID SHIT. BIG DEAL.
YEAH, BUT AT LEAST YOU WERE HORNY FOR THOSE OTHER GIRLS, SO THAT MADE IT EASIER.
JESUS... I NEVER SAID I WASN'T ATTRACTED TO MIKO, OKAY?
I WAS JUST... IDEALIZING WHAT I COULDN'T HAVE, YOU KNOW? IT HAPPENS.
MM-HMN.

89

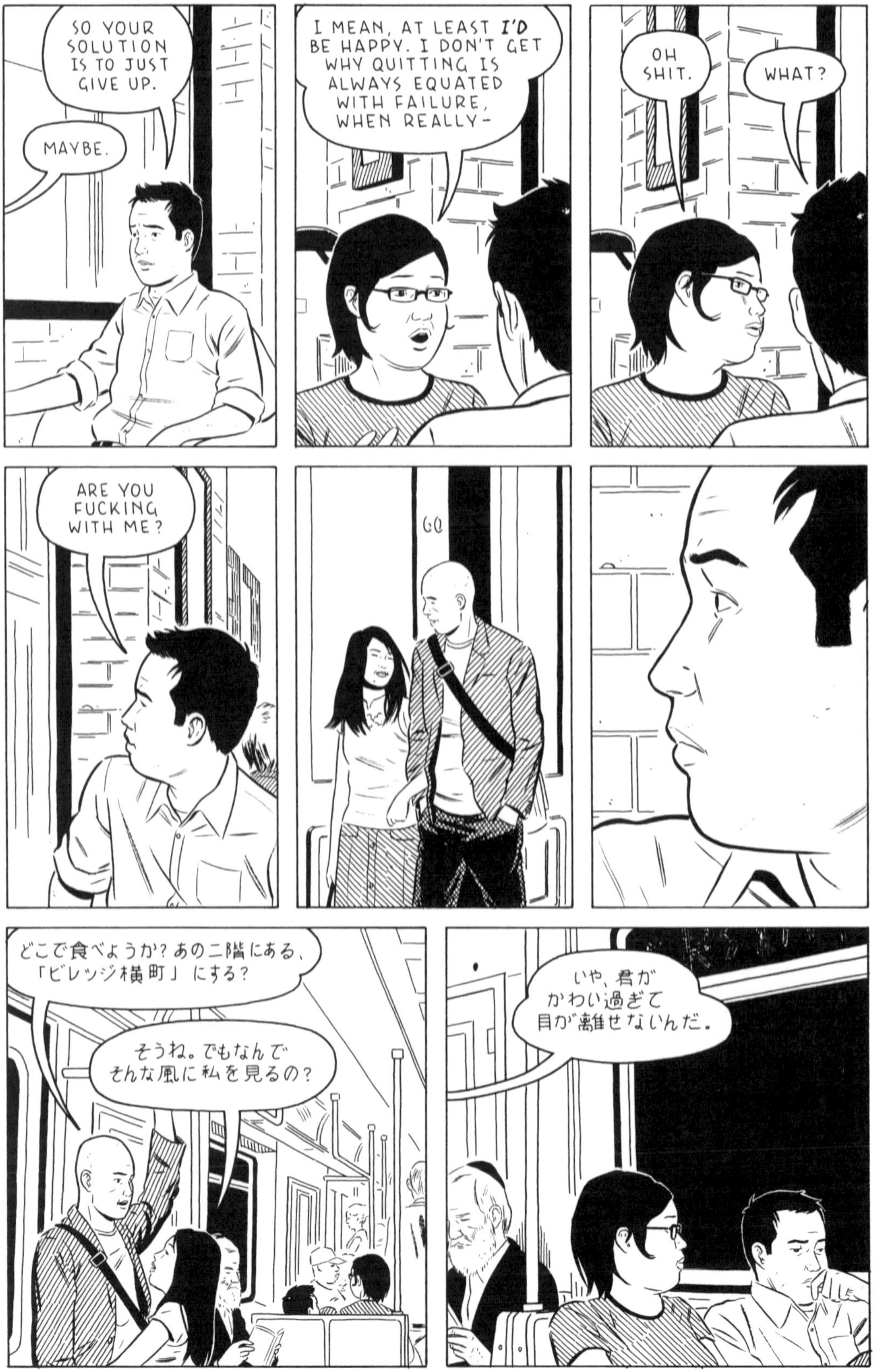
SO YOUR SOLUTION IS TO JUST GIVE UP.
MAYBE.
I MEAN, AT LEAST *I'D* BE HAPPY. I DON'T GET WHY QUITTING IS ALWAYS EQUATED WITH FAILURE, WHEN REALLY-
OH SHIT.
WHAT?
ARE YOU FUCKING WITH ME?
どこで食べようか？あの二階にある、「ビレッジ横町」にする？
そうね。でもなんでそんな風に私を見るの？
いや、君がかわい過ぎて目が離せないんだ。

92

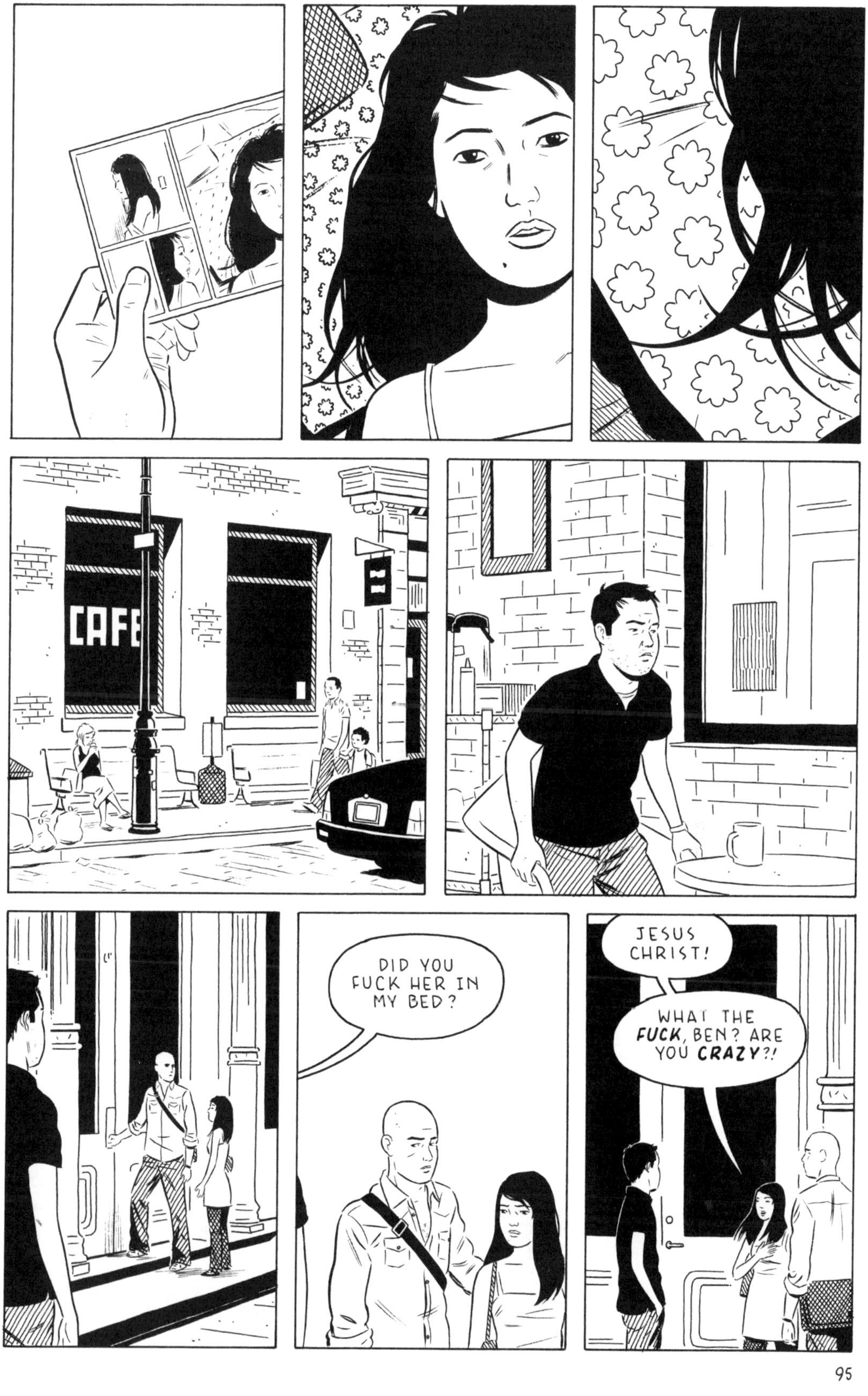
CAFE
DID YOU FUCK HER IN MY BED?
JESUS CHRIST!
WHAT THE **FUCK**, BEN? ARE YOU **CRAZY**?!

97

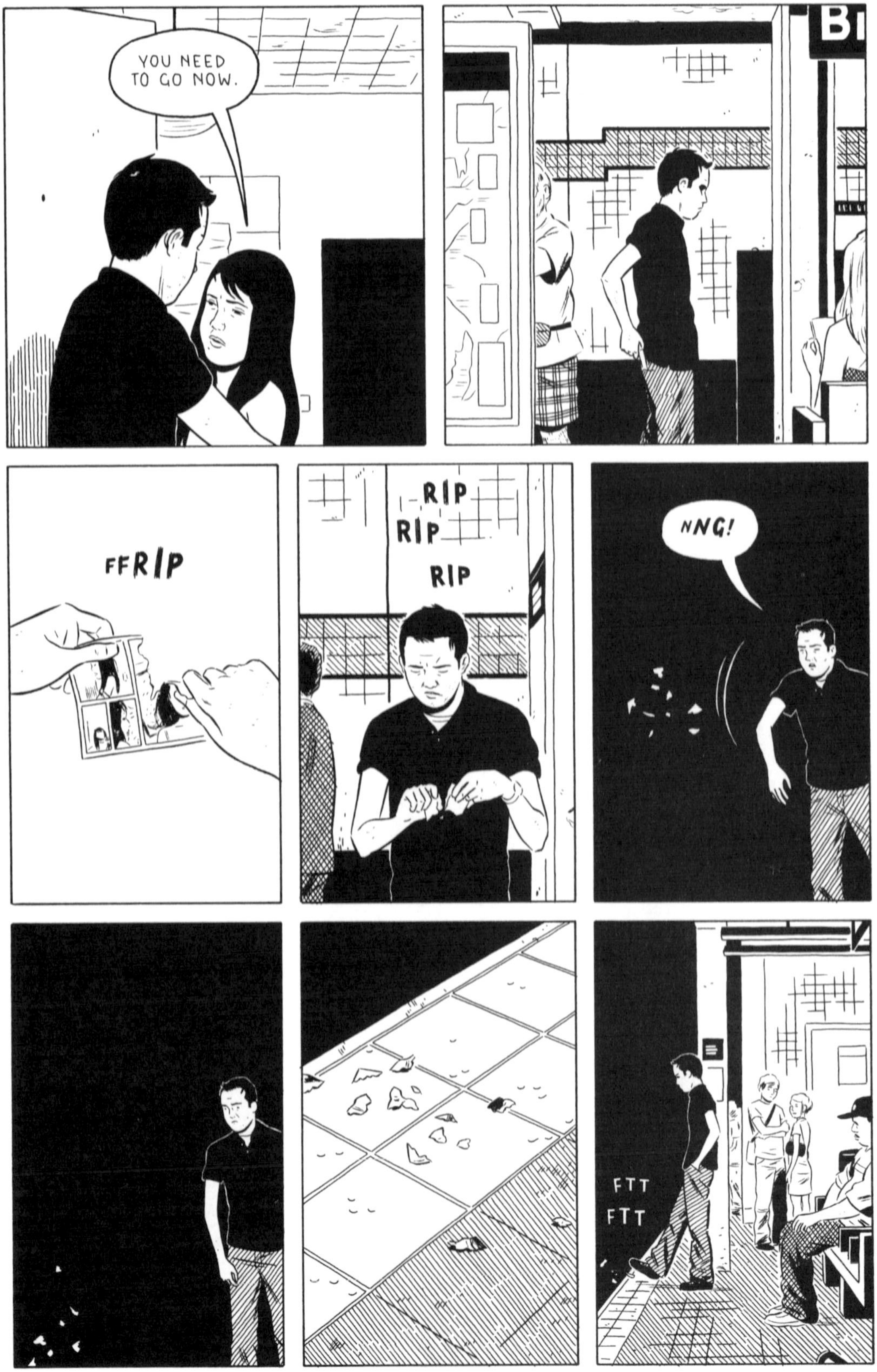
YOU NEED TO GO NOW.
FFRIP
RIP
RIP
RIP
NNG!
FTT
FTT

Since 1931

I JUST WANTED TO SAY "THANKS" TO EVERYONE FOR BEING HERE.

I DON'T KNOW IF TURNING THIRTY-TWO IS REALLY SOMETHING TO *CELEBRATE*, BUT I WILL STILL ALLOW YOU TO BUY ME DRINKS.

HA HA HA

UM...LAST MONTH I HAD THE GOOD FORTUNE OF CROSSING PATHS WITH AN OLD ACQUAINTANCE WHO WAS VISITING FROM CALIFORNIA...

AND I DON'T THINK IT'S ANY SECRET THAT I'VE SINCE FALLEN... HEAD OVER HEELS FOR HER.

SHE'S FALLING-DOWN DRUNK!

HA HA HA HA

AND JUST A FEW MINUTES AGO, SHE TOLD ME THAT SHE'S DECIDED TO MOVE HERE, AND THAT'S ABOUT THE BEST BIRTHDAY PRESENT I COULD IMAGINE.

CLAP CLAP CLAP CLA

SO KEEP BUYING ME DRINKS, BUT BUY ALICE A DRINK, TOO, AND WELCOME HER TO HER NEW HOME!

CLAP CLAP CL CLA

CLAP CLAP CLAP CLAP CLAP CLAP CL

CLAP CLAP CLAP CLAP CLA

105

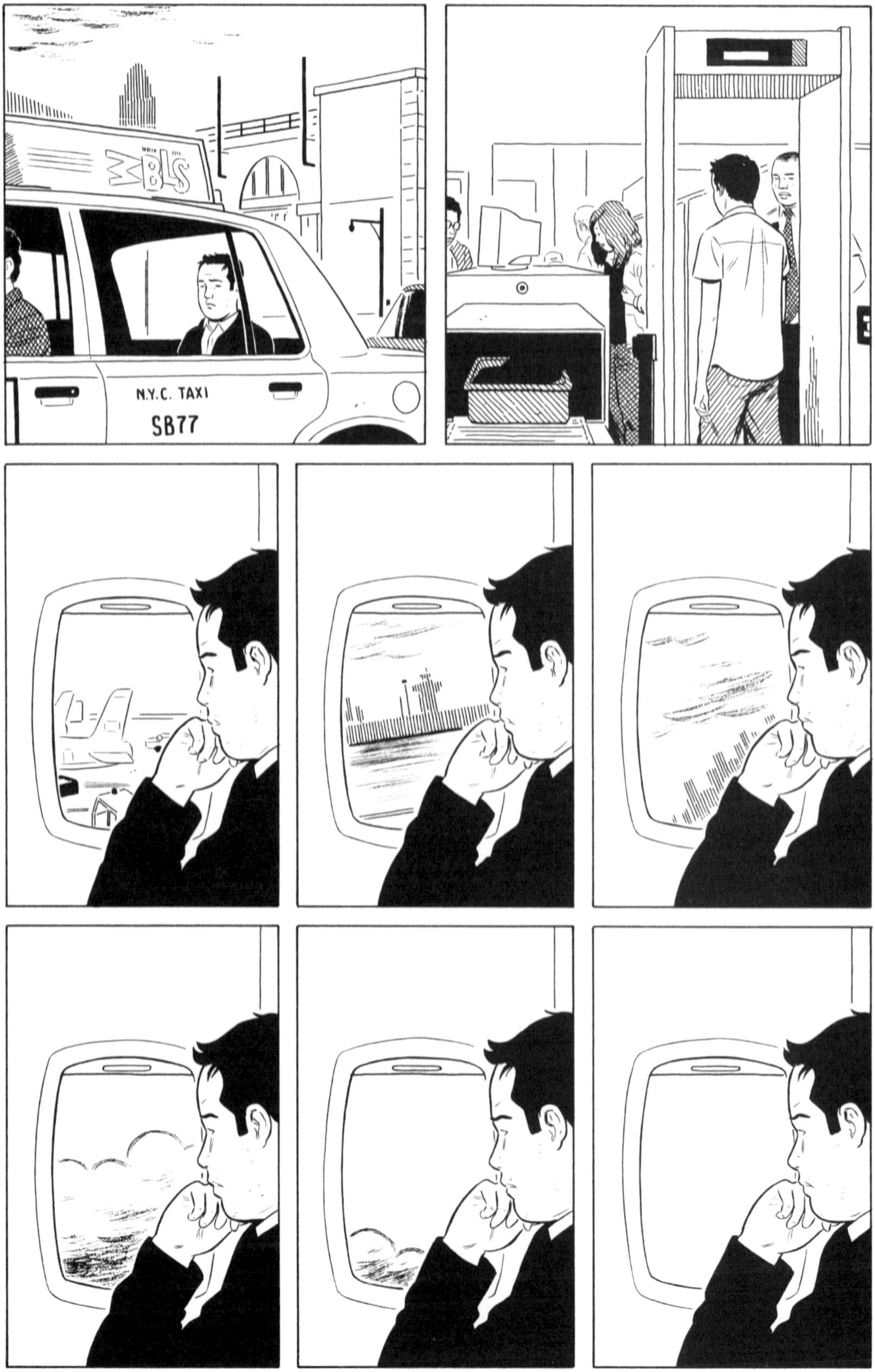
WBLS
N.Y.C. TAXI
SB77

ACKNOWLEDGMENTS

Thank you: Sarah Brennan, Peggy Burns, cartoonist pals, Tom
Devlin, Naomi Hyon, Sonjia Hyon, John Kuramoto, Taro Nettleton,
Chris Oliveros, Jamie Quail, Daniel Raeburn, Rebecca Rosen.